LIGHTHOUSE FAMILIES

CHERYL SHELTON-ROBERTS

BRUCE ROBERTS

Pineapple Press, Inc,
Sarasota, Florida

Inquiries should be addressed to:

Pineapple Press, Inc.
P.O. Box 3889
Sarasota, Florida 34230

www.pineapplepress.com

Library of Congress Cataloging-in-Publication Data

Shelton-Roberts, Cheryl.
    Lighthouse families / Cheryl Shelton-Roberts, Bruce Roberts. – Second edition.
        pages cm
    Summary: "New paperback edition of original hardback published by Crane Hill in 1997. A record of the memories and stories of America's lighthouse keepers. Descriptions of daily life at a lighthouse" – Provided by publisher.
    Summary: "A record of the memories and stories of America's lighthouse keepers and their children, who lived amid Fresnel lenses, spiral staircases, virulent storms, and daring rescues. Includes descriptions of daily life at a lighthouse by the people who grew up in these beacons" – Provided by publisher.
    ISBN 978-1-56164-631-9 (pbk.)
    1. Lighthouse keepers–United States–History. 2. Lighthouse keepers–Family relationships–United States. 3. Lighthouses–United States–History. I. Roberts, Bruce, 1930– II. Title.

VK1023.S495 2013
387.1'55092273–dc23
[B]

                                                                                                    2013020697

Printed in the United States

TABLE OF CONTENTS

To my mother,
Elizabeth Coatney Shelton
Cheryl Shelton-Roberts

To the thirteen families
who made this book
Bruce and Cheryl

OREWORD

Hundreds of business firms use lighthouses as part of their logos to symbolize strength and security, religious groups use them as a sign of hope in a troubled world, and consumers purchase reproductions and paintings of them to adorn their homes. People have always been fascinated by lighthouses, but suddenly that fascination has turned into frenzy. Why? The answer is simple—our lighthouses and their history are disappearing right before our eyes.

Lighthouses were built for one purpose only: to save lives. The magnitude of this effect on our nation's maritime history can never be measured. The beams of light from these noble beacons have saved countless lives, ships, and cargo. However, modern technology has put many of them out of business. Thanks to volunteers, historical groups, and communities, many of these venerable landmarks are now being saved and restored.

A good friend of mine, Ken Black, founder of the Shore Village Lighthouse Museum in Rockland, Maine, coined the phrase "Lighthouses are like people—they come in many different sizes, shapes, colors, and brightnesses." And that's what most of the lighthouse books published in the past twenty years have dealt with: the height of the towers, the power of the lenses, their ghost stories, famous keepers, and when the structures were built or destroyed. But few, until this book, have dealt with sincere and vivid personal memories of what lighthouse family life was really like, what lighthouses meant to the families then, and what lighthouses mean today.

Before the opportunity was nearly lost forever, Cheryl Shelton-Roberts and her husband, Bruce, undertook the monumental task of documenting and saving, for you and future generations, the memories and stories of the lighthouse family members still living. Through the profoundly captivating personal stories and photographs in *Lighthouse Families*, you will be introduced to a vital part of our nation's lighthouse history that until now has been unchronicled.

So sit back in your favorite chair, relax, and let your mind drift back to another era, another way of life. Start reading, and you, too, will soon become a member of the *Lighthouse Families*.

Timothy Harrison
Editor, *Lighthouse Digest*

U.S. Lighthouse Service exhibit at the 1926 Sesqui-Centennial Exposition in Philadelphia

In the late 1800s and the early 1900s, U.S. Lighthouse Service displays attracted lots of attention at exhibitions and centennials across the country. The service had gained a reputation for being on the cutting edge of navigational technology, the technology that ironically would eventually eliminate the need for human keepers. One of the last U.S. Lighthouse Service displays was exhibited at the 1926 Sesqui-Centennial Exposition in Philadelphia, and Bodie Island Keeper Vernon Gaskill was chosen as one of the lighthouse service representatives to man the display. (See the letter from the Superintendent of Lighthouses to Keeper Gaskill on page xi; for more about Keeper Vernon Gaskill and his family, see "Bodie Island: Home Is Where the Lighthouse Is," page 169.) Photograph courtesy of The National Archives

$\mathscr{I}$NTRODUCTION

$\mathbf{H}$undreds of them still stand. They have been attacked by Indians, shot at from land and sea, battered by hurricanes, placed under the care of stingy and dishonest bureaucrats, and abandoned as surplus relics. But for more than a century and a half, they have helped save thousands of lives, and America's lighthouses may represent the best money the United States government has ever spent, with the exception of the Louisiana Purchase.

From the coasts of Maine to the Florida Keys, up and around the Gulf to Texas, across the Great Lakes from the St. Lawrence River to the Apostle Islands, and from Mexico to British Columbia, stand the American continental lighthouses. They were built in isolated places such as Outer Island, in Lake Superior 30 miles from the Wisconsin shore; Tatoosh Island, 6 miles off the Washington coast; Passage Island, a six-hour boat ride from the American side of Lake Superior; and Saddleback Ledge, a rocky outcropping miles from the Maine coastline.

We look at lighthouses today and see symbols of solitude, endurance, hope, and caring. But there is another way of looking at them—we can look at them as "home." During the first part of the twentieth century light stations were home to more than 5,000 U.S. Lighthouse Service keepers and employees and their families. These are not people who seek attention for themselves—they are quiet people who lived under strict government rules and made family and work their top priorities. These behind-the-scenes heroes literally put their lives on the line to make America's coastal and inland waterways safe, a key factor in the development of our nation's lucrative and prolific shipping industry.

The government agency that constructed, maintained, and staffed America's light stations no longer exists. Its records are literally scattered about government archives, and the only visible symbol in Washington today is a small lighthouse carved in stone over a side entrance of the Department of Commerce Building on 19th Street.

The U.S. Light-House Board came into being in 1852 as the result of a reorganization when the supervision of lighthouses was removed by Congress from the discredited control of the fifth auditor of the U.S. Treasury Department. Under the scrutiny of professional engineers and maritime experts, the U.S. Light-House Board remained in authority until another reorganization in 1910 established the Bureau of Lighthouses led by some of the finest civilian leaders in lighthouse history, including Commissioner of Lighthouses George Putnam. The Bureau of Lighthouses remained in authority until control of the light stations passed to the U.S. Coast Guard as part of President Franklin

President Franklin Delano Roosevelt (far right), Lighthouse Superintendent William Demeritt (far left), and Key West and Miami officials at Bahia Honda Bridge in Key West, Florida, in February 1939, about four months before the Reorganization Act took effect in July

President Franklin Delano Roosevelt is shaking his fist at William Demeritt, superintendent of the Seventh District of the Bureau of Lighthouses and a former keeper of Key West Light Station. Superintendent Demeritt had caught wind of FDR's reorganization plan to end the U.S. Lighthouse Service per se and merge it with the U.S. Coast Guard. He told the president that he could not, absolutely could not do that. FDR angrily responded to Demeritt's demand to keep the U.S. Lighthouse Service intact and to communicate that he did what was necessary as president to protect the country's welfare. Photograph and legend courtesy of Key West Art and Historical Society and Monroe County Library in Key West

Delano Roosevelt's 1939 Reorganization Act. In general, prior to 1852 the national lighthouse authority was referred to as the U.S. Lighthouse Establishment; after 1852 it was known as the U.S. Lighthouse Service, although government documents show these terms used interchangeably.

After the much-needed 1852 reorganization, the U.S. Light-House Board equipped American lighthouses with Fresnel lenses, designed by Augustin Fresnel in France in the early 1820s. Fresnel lenses use prisms to refract and reflect light into a focused beam that reaches farther than the old curved silver reflectors. Amazingly, many of the Fresnel lenses installed before the Civil War are still in use. The key to their longterm success is their beehive open-center design that can accommodate everything from whale oil and kerosene lamps to electric bulbs. In the 1830s, a first-order lens, one of the largest Fresnel lenses, cost about $3,000; the value of the first-order lenses still in use at St. Augustine (Florida), Point Reyes (California), and other lighthouses is placed much higher.

In the last half of the nineteenth century, many cities held expositions to show off the latest advances in technology and science, and the U.S. Lighthouse Service's exhibits usually featured a large rotating Fresnel lens, always a crowd pleaser. But at the 1893 World's Columbian Exposition in Chicago, the lighthouse exhibitors strung thirteen electric buoys a half mile offshore and a half mile apart to define a channel between two shoals in Lake Michigan. The electric underwater cable that connected the lights was powered by a dynamo on shore—it was quite a sight for people who had lived all their lives with only a candle or oil lamp to light their nights.

But the exposition judges, impressed as they were, didn't give the electrically lit waterway an award—instead they awarded some new-style buoys, one of which whistled. The buoy filled itself with air while rising on a wave and then expelled the air through a whistle as it sank, giving a loud warning that could be heard around the clock in all weather conditions. And the whistling buoy required little maintenance, making it a tremendous advantage over buoys fitted with lamps and either fuel oil that had to be replenished or awkward glass jar batteries that had to be recharged every seventy-two hours.

In the 1920s lighthouse officials recognized radio navigation as the "wave" of the future, and by the time people were hearing the first commercial radio broadcasts, the Great Lakes were already networked by this latest technology. George Putnam, Commissioner of Lighthouses from the early 1900s until his retirement in 1935, documented in a 1936 *National Geographic* article the novel experiments in radio navigation lighthouse officials tried as early as 1901. Putnam stated that the preservation of old lighthouse towers, such as Navesink in New Jersey, which displayed the first two Fresnel lenses in America in 1841 and hosted the first wireless transmission by Guglielmo Marconi in 1899, would be fortunate as they often figured "prominently in local history and romance." He also believed that "our steady change to modern automated lights has saved the public much money. And for primary lights the maxim that 'Safety is found only in certainty' and human attention, given by light keepers, must be retained." Unfortunately Putnam's advice fell on deaf ears within the U.S. government.

In 1939, having survived the austerity of government cuts during the Great Depression, the U.S. Lighthouse Service merged into the U.S. Coast Guard under President Franklin Delano Roosevelt's Reorganization Act. Officially President Roosevelt said that economics prompted the merger, but many people suspected that he was trying to strengthen America's military forces without upsetting a Congress that was reluctant to get the nation involved in World War II. At President Roosevelt's directive, armed coastguardsmen manned all of the lighthouse stations to deter sabotage and defend the sites in case of enemy attack, which became a distinct possibility in 1942 when German submarines operated off the East Coast and later when Japanese submarines and destroyers approached the West Coast.

U.S. Coast Guard officials ordered young enlisted men assigned to lighthouse duty to clean out all of the old U.S. Lighthouse Service civilian artifacts and institute regulation military lifestyle. At Horton Point Light in New York, everything bearing the old U.S. Lighthouse Service name, including the antique wood and brass lighthouse clock, was tossed into Long Island Sound. At Split Rock Light on Lake Superior, brass oil-cans, dishes, and other items quickly disappeared, either destroyed or appropriated for personal use. At Key West Light Station, every brass, oak, and mahogany artifact was trashed beyond recovery. Finally realizing the turmoil and personal upset caused by the Reorganization Act, President Roosevelt issued an executive order that the light stations would always be accessible to the U.S. Lighthouse Service families who had lived at them—but the president's attempt at amends was too little, too late.

It can be argued that the first American casualties of World War II were the U.S. Lighthouse Service employees. For a hundred years lighthouse keepers and their families had been part of the American consciousness, and the names of those who had served above and beyond the call of duty, such as Abbie Burgess and Ida Lewis, had become household words. By the end of World War II, radio navigation outmoded the need for manned lighthouses, and the U.S. Coast Guard found itself with hundreds of neglected light station buildings it could not afford to maintain. Some of the buildings were sold to private individuals and others burned to discourage vandals. Items designated "junk," including small sixth-order Fresnel lenses, were considered too trivial to store and were dumped.

World War II was the defining life experience for a generation of Americans, and technological advances debuted at an ever-increasing rate. By 1950 the world was seeing more than a century of change every fifty years, by 1970 the pace had picked up to every twenty-five years, and by 1980, as Orson Wells predicted, a century of change was realized every ten years. Funding of new scientific and military developments took priority over preserving the past.

Now, more than a half century after Pearl Harbor, the U.S. Lighthouse Service has been all but forgotten. The U.S. Coast Guard has absorbed some of the lighthouse service's history by naming new cutters after women lighthouse keepers and including these female heroes in their official annals. In recent years the National Park Service has stepped in to help preserve about thirty-five of the most beautiful and famous light-

DEPARTMENT OF COMMERCE

BUREAU OF LIGHTHOUSES

WASHINGTON   May 17, 1939.

Mr. L. V. Gaskill,
Bodie Island Light Station,
Wanchese, North Carolina.

Dear Mr. Gaskill:

In reply to your letter of May 15, 1939, I can only ad-
vise you that the conflicting rumors to which you refer
are doubtless a reflection from the present uncertainty as
to the ultimate working out of the administrative set-up
which will result from the pending Reorganization Order.
Conferences are now in progress on this general subject, the
ultimate results of which may not be known for several weeks.
You will appreciate that the merger of two activities, one
of which is organized along military lines and the other
along purely civilian lines, will not be a simple matter to
work out, and that such changes as may be made may be pro-
gressive and gradual rather than complete at one time.
The ultimate authority in such matters will, of course, rest
in the Treasury Department and upon recommendation of the
Commandant of the Coast Guard rather than with this office,
since it appears quite within the realm of probability or
at least possibility that the existence of the Lighthouse
Service as a separate entity of the Government may cease
when this Order takes effect.

Please accept my best wishes for the future well-being
of yourself and many other loyal employees of the Lighthouse
Service with whom it has been my pleasure to serve during the
best part of a life-time.

Sincerely yours,

Commissioner of Lighthouses.

HDK:EBF

Letter from the commissioner of lighthouses in response to Keeper Vernon Gaskill's questions about the merger of the U.S. Lighthouse Service with the U.S. Coast Guard

Fearful rumors and distrust rippled through the ranks of lighthouse keepers all over America when President Franklin Delano Roosevelt's 1939 Reorganization Act gave the U.S. Coast Guard responsibility for the nation's light stations. Concerned about the future of his career, Principal Keeper Vernon Gaskill had written to Commissioner of Lighthouses Harold King about the rumors he had heard. Document courtesy of the Gaskill family (For more about Keeper Vernon Gaskill and his family, see "Bodie Island: Home Is Where the Lighthouse Is," page 169.)

house towers. And local historical and nonprofit groups are also working to rescue and preserve these unique architectural treasures that visually crown the land around them.

While the future of light station buildings looks relatively secure, the memories of the U.S. Lighthouse Service and the families and children who called lighthouse keepers' dwellings "home" are still in jeopardy of being lost forever. That's why we compiled this book. We spent more than five years seeking out and talking with "children," now in their sixties, seventies, eighties, and nineties, who grew up working alongside their keeper fathers and mothers. These children watched and helped their parents run personal marathons to keep the lights burning night after night under sometimes unbelievably difficult circumstances. For these children, isolation was a given, injury and death was a daily threat, distance from medical help was a part of life, self-sufficiency within the family unit was mandatory, and fulfillment was a well-lit, carefully tended beacon that pierced the fog and darkness and helped mariners find safe passage along America's shores.

Here, for the first time ever, is a collection of firsthand stories of children and families who called a light station "home."

ABOUT THE AUTHORS

CHERYL SHELTON-ROBERTS is cofounder and former president of the Outer Banks Lighthouse Society. She continues as vice president of the society and has been editor of the society's publication, *Lighthouse News*, for nearly twenty years. She was a classroom teacher in North Carolina and Virginia for two decades before retiring to work alongside her husband, Bruce, in their lighthouse specialty store and to produce books about lighthouses. To research this book, Cheryl and Bruce traveled across America from coast to coast gathering information about light stations, and Cheryl has made a special effort to seek out any living descendants of the keepers who served at these historic outposts. "Lighthouses are much like people in that the structures represent the humane quality of man caring for fellowman. I hear the voices of the past and feel the rhythms of life in them. I am awed not only by their architectural beauty but also by the stories of the people who kept the lights burning through countless storms and humdrum days to help make America's coastlines safe for everyone passing by."

BRUCE ROBERTS, a former director of photography and senior photographer of *Southern Living* magazine, began his photojournalism career at *The Tampa Tribune* and in the early 1960s became one of the legendary Charlotte (North Carolina) *Observer* staffers. Bruce's photographs have also appeared in *Sports Illustrated, Time, Life,* and Time Life Books, as well as *The Face of North Carolina, You Can't Kill the Dream,* and *Where Time Stood Still: A Portrait of Appalachia,* which was picked by *The New York Times* as one of the best children's books for 1970. Bruce has coauthored six bestselling lighthouse books and three popular historical books: *Plantation Homes of the James River, American Country Stores,* and *Steel Ships & Iron Men.* Bruce has won numerous international, national, and state awards, and some of his photographs are in the permanent collection of the Smithsonian Institution.

ACKNOWLEDGMENTS

When we began this project in 1992, we had no idea what a gift meeting these lighthouse children would be. Humble and not given to sensationalism or exaggeration, these people are reluctant to talk about themselves or their family experiences, but as they began to feel comfortable with us, they opened their hearts and minds and photo albums. Since most lighthouse families lived on remote stations and did not own cameras, photographs were often done in the nearest large town by a professional, which makes the pictures in this book precious and rare. We thank each of these lighthouse children for so graciously and generously entrusting us with their memories and treasured family photographs.

We also thank Ken Black of Shore Village Museum in Rockland, Maine, and Tim Harrison, owner of Lighthouse Depot in Maine and editor of Lighthouse Digest, for giving us the initial encouragement to start this project. And a special thank you to Tim for writing the Foreword for this book.

Thank you also to Cullen Chambers, a lighthouse restoration expert currently working at Tybee Island Light Station in Georgia, for his enthusiasm; to Nelson Morosini, of the Department of Parks and Recreation at Año Nuevo State Reserve at Pigeon Point Lighthouse in California, for introducing us to Herman Jaehne; to Dewey Livingston, a National Park Service historian, who sent us his excellent report on California's Point Reyes Light Station; to Steve Harrison, a historian at Manteo Headquarters of Cape Hatteras National Seashore in North Carolina, for sharing his wealth of information with us; and to Dave Snyder, a National Park Service historian, for his help in contacting keepers' children in the Apostle Islands National Lakeshore area.

And finally, a hearty thank you to our family members and business staff for picking up the pieces for us when we were traveling and working to complete this book.

Although many of the lighthouse family members in this book have crossed the bar, their stories remain part of history. Every year we lose direct connections with American lighthouses not only because U.S. Lighthouse Service keepers are gone but also because their children are disappearing as well. As you read, listen to their voices tell amazing stories about living at a light station and smile with them at the incredible odds of surviving olden days without electricity, antibiotics, or nearby medical help. Theirs was a time of few roads, and a device such as a television—let alone a cell phone—was merely a vision of a distant future. These people lived by the rules of nature and the grace of God. The entire focus of their lives was a light that was in excellent working order to reach seaward and serve those who needed them.

$\mathscr{L}$IGHTHOUSE $\mathscr{F}$AMILIES

POINT ARENA

SIX DAUGHTERS AT A LIGHTHOUSE

When William "Bill" Owens retired in 1963, he had served a total of thirty-three years as a lighthouse keeper. He was the last of the U.S. Lighthouse civilian keepers on the West Coast who had been absorbed by the U.S. Coast Guard in the 1939 merger, and he received the Gallatin Award, the highest award that can be given to a federal civilian employee. Bill and his wife, Cora Isabel, already had three young daughters, Shirley, Sarah Lou, and Dixie, when he received his first keeper's assignment at Point Conception. While in service there from 1931 until 1935, their twins, Jean and Joan, were born. Concerned about his children's education, Keeper Owens hoped for an opening at Point Sur Light Station, which had good schools close by, but in June 1937 a more desirable position opened—the keeper's job at Point Arena Light Station. So the Owens family packed up and moved to what some consider paradise, and in 1939 the sixth Owens daughter was born in the Point Arena keeper's house.

Keeper Owens had his hands full in more ways than one at Point Arena Light Station. Maintaining the lighthouse, with its powerful first-order Fresnel lens, made great demands on the keeper, and raising six daughters maturing through their teen years with virile coastguardsmen nearby made additional demands. Like all families, the Owenses had their share of joys as well as trials. Isabel and all six of the girls kept journals that provide wonderful details about day-to-day life at Point Arena, including the number of steps in the tower—which varies depending on who was doing the counting! The journals also tell about the Owens family seeing World War II military events several times right in their own "backyard"—events the U.S. government has never confirmed.

One of the most bizarre battles of World War II took place within sight and sound of Point Arena Lighthouse. By the summer of 1945 the Americans had destroyed the major Japanese cities, and the Japanese Imperial Command desperately needed a face-saving "victory" they could report to the discouraged Japanese people. They came up with a wild and daring plan to invade the U.S. mainland. The once-proud Japanese Navy could muster only three destroyers for this last attack, but they loaded them with troops and sent them toward Point Arena.

The Japanese chose Point Arena as their landing place because it is on a remote stretch of the northern California coast miles from major military protection. Everyone, including the Japanese, knew that an invasion would have been a temporary victory at best, but it offered Japanese naval personnel a chance to demonstrate their pride and patriotism, as the kamikazes had done earlier in the war.

U.S. officials evidently learned about the planned "save-face landing on the beach between the Garcia River and Alder Creek," as Keeper Owens is quoted in an April 14, 1977, issue of the *Mendocino Beacon*. The U.S. government did not make the impending assault public, but Keeper Owens did receive a dispatch ordering him to have all available cars parked in front of the lighthouse and to be prepared to evacuate his family at a moment's notice. From then on, all six girls slept downstairs with their parents so they could leave literally at a moment's notice.

Bill Owens in the army during World War I
Bill witnessed World War I as a soldier and World War II as the keeper of a lighthouse threatened by Japanese submarines and destroyers. Photograph courtesy of the Owens family

About 9 p.m. on August 12, 1945, two days before the end of the war, Keeper Bill Owens heard the sound of battle offshore. Isabel and the girls awoke, and the whole family watched the flashes of guns on the horizon and felt the house shake with each repercussion. The U.S. Navy never released an account of what happened that night, but the Owens family knows. As Bill told a reporter from the *Mendocino Beacon* decades later, "Three Japanese destroyers tried to come ashore, but the navy was waiting on them. A week later the beach was covered with blankets and blood plasma bags and Japanese rice bowls and sandals. That stuff never got in the papers."

How the U.S. Navy learned that Point Arena would be the target remains a mystery. It is well-known that the Japanese codes had been broken earlier in the war, and one theory suggests that the navy picked up radio transmissions about the planned invasion.

Isabel Owens proudly presents baby Diana
Diana's older sister Jean recorded in her journal, "In 1939 I was five years old when a midwife came to live with us. I do believe I was quite unaware of what was really going to happen. I remember how Dad had to keep the old coal stove heated so the baby could be brought into the kitchen to be washed and wrapped in blankets. Dad kept telling us to keep the kitchen door shut so the heat would stay. Finally the event took place, and I remember the midwife bringing this new baby into the kitchen. The baby was called Diana." Photograph courtesy of the Owens family

Another theory suggests that surrender negotiations had been under way before the attack began, but the destroyers left Japan without radios and could not be recalled. Another theory suggests that Japanese negotiators may have revealed the planned attack so the U.S. Navy could stop any resulting casualties. Perhaps the Owens family had been saved by revelations by the Japanese themselves.

Not only had Keeper Bill Owens witnessed the last sea battle of World War II, but he had also spotted one of the first Japanese submarines in 1941 two days after the start of the war. Joan, one of the twin daughters born in 1933, wrote in her journal, "In 1941, shortly after Pearl Harbor, my father reported seeing a Japanese submarine not too far from the lighthouse. When he reported it to the district office, he was told that it could not be possible and for him to go back to bed. A couple of nights later one of our oil tankers, the *Montebello*, was torpedoed north of us."

All of the Owens girls recorded memories of World War II in their journals, but Joan's thoughts seem especially poignant. "It was a little tense for a while as things were happening too close to home. Anytime I saw a ship on the ocean, I would wonder if it was our ship or the Japanese. My mother moved my sisters and me from upstairs to a downstairs bedroom next to theirs. At different intervals we would get orders from the coast guard office to put up blackout curtains on the windows. It always made us feel

like we were hiding from the unknown, always suspecting the worst. There were times during the blackouts when the roaring sound of airplanes going directly over us would be almost deafening. We would all sit in silence wondering, 'Are they ours or are they theirs?'

"Near the end of the war, my father received orders from the office to keep the car filled with gas at all times and ready to go in case of an evacuation. I remember going out on our front porch one evening and looking out across the ocean. I could see flashes of light in the distance on the horizon. It was fascinating to watch, but after learning it had been a sea battle, it gave me an uneasy feeling. I had nightmares for years after that–I would always dream the Japanese would be climbing up the cliffs and we would have to escape out of the house and hide in the cistern by the light tower. Thank heaven the nightmares diminished with age."

Diana, who was born in 1939, wrote about the later war years. "During World War II, I have vivid memories of an alert coming through of possible enemy planes or ships in the area and we'd have to put up blackout shades on the windows. To this day I don't understand why we did all that, though, because the light on the tower had to stay lit and as the light swept around, the houses and surrounding area were in full view."

Dixie, born in 1930, wrote, "The parents of our girlfriends who lived in town would not let them spend the night with us because we were so close to the ocean. They seemed to think the Japanese would land."

Shirley, born in 1927, recorded, "We were notified to be ready to leave at a moment's notice. I don't remember, or even if I knew, where we were to go. I also wondered why the light beacon was on. And since the houses were on the other side of the light from the ocean, if an enemy ship shelled the light and missed, we would be hit."

Mother Isabel wrote, "In time of war the coast guard automatically is placed under the jurisdiction of the navy. It then became necessary for civilian keepers to enlist in a military service, at least for the duration of the war as they would not keep civilians on any of their installations. After considerable correspondence Bill joined the coast guard

reserve with the understanding he would remain at Point Arena and could return to his civilian keeper status after the war. He enlisted October 6, 1942.

"The war changed things quite a bit. Since the West Coast is closest to Japan, there were three systems of watches. The lighthouse crew had to report by phone to San Francisco

ABOVE: Diana Owens in front of her childhood home at Point Arena

Diana, the youngest of the six Owens girls, was born and grew up in the keeper's house at Point Arena. "It was the happiest time of my life," Diana fondly remembers. "It made me who I am today, a secure person due to a strong family and all the opportunities to explore and analyze things for myself." Photograph courtesy of the Owens family

LEFT: (Back row, from left) Sarah Lou, Dixie, and Shirley; (front row, from left) Joan and Jean
The five older Owens girls plus "baby" Diana made for a full keeper's house at Point Arena. Photograph courtesy of the Owens family

The view from the Point Arena Lighthouse catwalk during World War II
The Owens lived in the house in the forefront, and the single coastguardsmen

everything sighted on the ocean or in the air. There was a civilian watch about one mile from the lighthouse. And a group of about thirty soldiers lived at the station temporarily while they set up barracks for them elsewhere. They stayed in some empty houses. They rode horses to keep watch along the coast. They always had one man riding south and another riding north.

"A plane came in low over the station. The pilot made the sign that he was in trouble. Bill and another man watched as it came down in a field that had just been plowed–the

stationed at Point Arena during World War II lived right next door. Keeper Owens tried to keep a distance between his six attractive daughters and the young men, but even so, four of the coastguardsmen who arrived going with other girls changed their minds and married Owens girls instead. Photograph courtesy of the Owens family

plane hit the ground, went up on its nose, and then settled back down. Bill and the other man rushed over to it. The pilot was not injured. He said he had run out of fuel. Bill called the district office and was told to keep a twenty-four-hour watch on the plane. It had the Norden Bomb Sight, a new invention, and they didn't want anyone to see or get it."

The Norden Bomb Sight became one of the most important inventions of World War II, giving the advantage to Allied bombers over Europe. Keeper Owens kept a

USO personnel arrive at Point Arena during World War II
During World War II, USO (United Service Organizations) personnel periodically provided entertainment for the keeper's family and coastguardsmen at the light station. Photograph courtesy of the Owens family

double-barreled shotgun at the lighthouse for vermin such as rattlesnakes and infiltrating enemy. One can picture his alert, protective stance as he guarded the plane until help arrived.

For years there has been debate about how many Japanese submarines came to the West Coast and how close they got. Isabel didn't know how many—but she did know they were right in her backyard. She recorded, "One morning Bill was going on watch, he saw something about a mile off the coast. He thought it was a sub but wasn't sure. He called in to report it and was told by the officer of the day, 'There are no subs in these waters, go back to bed.' I also saw it as I was washing the dishes. A day or so later a Japanese sub sank a lumber schooner north of the station. The next day some officers came to swear Bill to secrecy. Bill wanted to know how long they wanted him to keep quiet about it and was told, 'Until after the war.'

"A few miles south of Point Arena was the Olson Sheep Ranch. Mr. Olson was riding his horse around the ranch, and as he got close to the bluff he heard a humming noise. He rode closer and saw a Japanese sub sitting in close to the bluff, apparently recharging the batteries. He called the district office from the lighthouse to report it. They sent a plane up to bomb it. The first bomb missed; the second went down the hatch. That was the end of that submarine. One or two days after the sinking the newspaper printed pictures of two types of Japanese subs. One of them was exactly like what I'd seen from the kitchen window of the lighthouse.

"Bill had orders from the district office that all cars on the station should be full of gas and loaded with food and blankets. All women and children should be ready to evacuate. We prepared and had all the children sleep downstairs that night. But no call to evacuate came. I never heard if there really was a chance of an invasion or if it was for practice.

"Within one or two days of the end of the war there was a battle at sea, south of Point Arena. We couldn't see the ships but we could hear the guns and see the flashes

The Owens family and the coastguardsmen based at the light station waiting to watch a USO movie
Keeper Owens and his family joined the coastguardsmen in their barracks to watch the movies supplied by the USO. It was quite a treat for the girls. Photograph courtesy of the Owens family

from them. The house would shake as the guns went off. There was also an incident with a zeppelin. It passed so low and so close that it brushed against the tower. Bill could see and hear the men laughing and talking. It got farther up the coast and for some unknown reason went down into the ocean and all men were lost."

The end of World War II did not bring an end to the excitement at Point Arena Light Station, and while the U.S. government had clamped censorship on all World War II military action at the point, a flurry of publicity accompanied other newsworthy events. Isabel closely details one such event. "Upon rising on the morning of September 9, 1949, we saw there was a very thick fog, and the station's foghorn had been blowing for some time. We could barely see the fog-signal building from our kitchen.

"Then we heard a ship blowing for fog. Each blast sounded closer and closer until it sounded like it was in our backyard. Bill suddenly left the breakfast table to go see if something was wrong. He was in time to hear the crash. They had struck Wash Rock, about a mile from the point. They backed off, went forward again, and got solidly stuck. It was a British ship of the Furnace Line, the *Pacific Enterprise,* a passenger and freight ship.

"Bill called the lifeboat station and the district office. In the meantime, the fog began to lift until the ship could be seen. The lifeboat station sent their boat and men out to see what needed to be done. It was in no immediate danger of sinking so the crew was allowed to stay aboard. It stayed there for a couple of days with the waves pounding it.

"By about the third day there were signs of it breaking up so the coast guard ordered everybody off. The passengers were taken to the San Francisco immigration office. The crew ran up the black ball, which indicated it was not abandoned. The ship was insured by Lloyds of London. In case of a shipwreck the fog chart has to be sent to the district office because it shows when the horn was blowing. The pilot had thought they were near the Farallon Islands. The captain of the ship was on his last trip before retiring.

OPPOSITE PAGE, INSET: Keeper Bill Owens and his wife, Cora Isabel, about 1945

During the last months of World War II, American officials learned that the Japanese planned to make a face-saving invasion of the United States. With remote Point Arena a probable enemy landing site, Keeper Owens was instructed to make sure his car was fueled and parked in front of the lighthouse ready to evacuate his family at a moment's notice. The night of August 12, 1945, two days before the Japanese surrendered, the family watched the flashes from guns in a sea battle just off the point. A few days later they found blankets, blood plasma bags, and Japanese rice bowls and sandals on the beach in front of the lighthouse. The U.S. Navy has never acknowledged the battle. "Three Japanese destroyers tried to come ashore, but the U.S. Navy was waiting on them," Bill Owens told a Mendocino Beacon reporter decades later. Photograph courtesy of the Owens family

Point Arena Light Station as it appeared during World War II
Photograph courtesy of the Owens family

The Point Arena first-order bull's-eye lens, with the primary and backup 1,000-watt quartz bulbs

Several ports had given him parties to celebrate, but this tragedy hit him so hard that he had a breakdown. Some people thought he would lose his retirement pension. We never heard the outcome."

The pilot and captain were not the only ones disturbed by the unfortunate event, according to Isabel's account. "Crowds flocked to the station to see it. Bill and rest of the station crew had their hands full keeping people from walking too close to the bluffs. A friend had brought a box of peaches to us. It had to stay on the porch because I was waxing floors just inside the door. Diana, about ten years old, saw a chance to make some money and was selling peaches at ten cents each to people walking by."

Joan also wrote about the shipwreck. "The news reporters did a lot of filming, and it was exciting when the film was shown at our little theater in Point Arena. My dad was shown being interviewed by the reporters, and I couldn't help feeling like a celebrity."

Isabel tells about the final moments of the ship. "As I was on my way to the barn to milk the cow the next day, I heard a loud whistling sound. I turned to see what it was and saw an air tank break out of the side of the ship and float south. The next day I saw the bow of the ship listing. Later that day I saw it break and go under the water.

The next morning the rest of the ship was gone.

"Some of the cargo floated onto the beaches. There were cans of snuff and salmon, hundred-pound sacks of flour, and much lumber. The flour got about one inch of crust, but inside it was dry. People came out every day to see what they could find on the beaches. The lumber was picked up by a rancher, but that was too valuable to let go. He was given a choice of paying for it or giving it up. A rug washed in. One of the coast-guardsmen found it and was going to cut it up to put on the floor of his car. I offered him five dollars for it instead, and he accepted."

The girls loved gathering things on the beach too, but in a more casual manner. Jean wrote in her journal, "Every spare moment Joan and I were at the beach behind the house looking for shells, eels, or anything else we might come upon. While Joan and I were at the beach one day at very low tide, our father was there with some abalone fishermen. They were having very poor luck. Dad looked at them and said that his twins could do much better than they had done, and he proceeded to hand us a crowbar to pry abalone from the rocks. Joan and I had never pried an abalone loose from the rocks in our lives, but we knew we couldn't let Dad down after he had just boasted to those men. So we proceeded out onto the rocks, and I'll never get over the surprise at finding a large abalone quite near the beach. We quickly shoved the crowbar behind the muscle of the abalone, before it could tighten its grip on the rock, and popped it loose. How exciting it all was! How proud we were as we marched up to the beach to show Dad and those city slickers."

"Several times in my life I have gotten myself into dire predicaments while at the beach," Jean noted in her journal. "Each time I was alone. Once

The Owens twins, Jean and Joan, and Diana playing with Pal, about 1944

Pal "found" the six Owens girls when he was a puppy and became their constant companion. Pal was fatally injured in a fall off the treacherous cliffs of Point Arena, one of the few very sad memories from an otherwise happy, adventuresome childhood. Photograph courtesy of the Owens family

15

(From left) Sarah, Dixie, and Joan
Like other lighthouse children, the Owens girls learned to be resourceful in making playthings. Makeshift stilts and roller skates provided hours of fun. Photograph courtesy of the Owens family

I had decided to go down this little path on the cliff by the front of the house. It didn't seem so precarious at the time, but as I turned around to go back up, I experienced this sinking feeling in the pit of my stomach as I looked at the narrow sandy path and then down below to the rushing water. I knew that no one would hear me call for help, plus the pride of needing to accomplish this feat on my own dominated. Need I say anything about my embarrassment of Mom and Dad finding out I could get myself into such a dangerous and ridiculous predicament? I sat for, I feel, an eternity, knowing I had to solve the problem myself. I decided to crawl up on my hands and knees. I did manage to reach the top with no great mishap, and to this day I consider it a well-learned, well-earned lesson."

Joan, like Jean, felt drawn to the sea. "My favorite pastime was going to the beach. We would explore the caves and walk the beaches looking for unusual shells and Japanese glass balls. Nearly every home in Point Arena had at least one glass ball that had floated in on the current.

"We had three big trees growing next to the house where Jean and I spent a lot of time. We made a makeshift tree house and could snuggle up among the branches out of the wind with a beautiful view of the ocean. It was comforting to sit there and watch the waves and talk and dream.

"My sisters and I," Joan continued, "spent a lot of time outdoors. We played kick the can, did a lot of roller-skating on the sidewalk, and played croquet and badminton. I doubt that we spent our time any differently than the town kids. The only difference was that they were confined in town where we had the wide open spaces.

"Building bonfires on the beach was not only fun but necessary. They kept us warm, and we enjoyed roasting potatoes. Sometimes it would take an hour to get a good fire going when we had the wind and fog working against us. I can remember building fires

The keeper's house at Point Arena Light Station
The surrounding natural beauty and endless possibilities of finding something new every day made Point Arena a special home for the Owens girls. Pal went with them everywhere. Photograph courtesy of the Owens family

too close to the surf only to have the waves douse them. Being young and patient, we would scoop everything up and start over again away from the tide. We would put the potatoes in the ashes and then just sit in front of the warm fire watching and listening to the surf. In the evenings, if the sky was clear, we would lay back and try to pick out the different constellations. When we tired of that, we would scoop the potatoes out of the fire and have our feast. Done or not, it was time to eat and head for home."

Sarah Lou, the second-oldest girl, born in 1928, expressed her fascination with Point Arena Lighthouse and their oceanside home. "There was a cave you could go into at low tide—we would slide down the clay and dirt bank to the beach. One day I decided to take my twin sisters, Jean and Joan, over the cliff to a small beach. I got them down okay, but I couldn't get them back up. I told them to stay put as I went up the cliff and went to the fog-signal building, got one of the ropes, and hurried back. I threw the rope over, told each of them what to do, and hauled them up. I then hurriedly wound the rope back up and put it away. We never told our parents about this until about four years prior to our father's death."

Sarah Lou's story is affirmed by her adoring sister Jean's written accounts. "Perhaps my mother wondered at these happenings as we certainly did not inform her of everything. I can recall my twin and I going down over the cliff with our older sister Sarah.

(From left) Sarah Lou, Jean, Dixie, Joan, and Shirley
The Owens girls often posed on the front steps of the keeper's house for family pictures.
Photograph courtesy of the Owens family

We had walked along the rocks and beaches to another cliff with a ladder to go back up. Meanwhile the tide had come in so we were unable to retrace our steps. We were then faced with the dilemma of not being able to reach the ladder. So I'm sure with much anxiety, Sarah had to leave us there while she went up the cliff to get a rope to pull us up to reach the ladder. We were not frightened, but I can well imagine Sarah was. We all survived the ordeal, but my mother never knew what had happened until about thirty years later when Sarah was reminiscing with Mom. Shocked is hardly a sufficient word!"

The girls' clothes required special attention after adventures like that. Ironing day was known as "Black Tuesday," according to Jean. "That day came around faster than any other day, and I just dreaded it. Now that I think back, I realize Mom probably dreaded it more than any of us. She ironed on one board, while my sisters and I took turns on two others."

Like all lighthouse parents serving on remote stations, Keeper Owens and Isabel often worried about the time when their children might need a doctor. Sarah Lou recorded what usually happened when one of them did not feel well. "The kitchen was the coziest room in the house. It had a coal stove, which was going all day and night. When one of us was sick, we would get to sit in our Morris chair (with an adjustable back and loose cushions) close to the stove. The cure-all was toast, warm milk, and the chair."

Being the parents of six daughters meant that Bill and Isabel also worried about boyfriends. Jean wrote about how her dad put distance between her and one of the young military men living near the light station. "One night when my mother had gone into town and Dad was sleeping on the couch ... or so I thought he was sleeping ... I found it a perfect time to visit Ed, my boyfriend, in the lighthouse watch room. It was dark and slightly foggy as I decided to take the path near the bluffs, so no one would see me, as we were not allowed in the watch room. After being very foolhardy by walking so close to the bluffs at night, I did manage to arrive at my destination intact. As I opened the door, I could not believe my eyes—my father was standing in the watch room next to Ed. Even to this day I do not know how he knew I had a rendezvous with Ed or how he managed to arrive before I did! It certainly confirmed my belief that parents are psychic."

Diana wrote about some of her special memories of Point Arena. "When I was about five or six, Jean and I gathered some articles from home, put them in a wooden barrel, and took it to the beach. We climbed up a cliff to put the barrel in a small alcove we had seen. Our purpose was to cover the barrel with sand and dirt and have it discovered years and years later as a great treasure. Of course the first storm washed it all away. I don't remember what we found to put in it, but I'm sure things were missing around the house that had people mystified for a while.

"Every night after dishes were done, my mother and I would go for a walk up the road. Our dog, Pal, always went with us—in fact he went everywhere on the station that any of us kids were going. By the time Mom and I would start on our walk, it was usually dusk or dark. Being out in the country, there were no lights except for the beam from the light tower that would cross our path every few seconds. We had a large cattle ranch bordering the station, so we could hear the cattle moving about on one side of us and sea lions and the ocean on the other side. "Mom would point out all the constellations to me on those walks. With no street lights and the air so clear, they were easy to see. Those walks with Mom and the closeness they created are a very special part of my childhood.

"In the wintertime during the storms," Diana continued, "I'd lay in bed at night and I could hear the waves beating the bluff and splashing against the banks. With some of the stronger storms I could see the water splashing over the banks, and to me that was a beautiful sight. One time during a strong wind, I decided it would be exciting to go out walking in it. Mom didn't realize I'd gone outside, but I was walking up the yard hanging onto the pickets of the fence as I went along. Dad happened to come along in the truck and saw me. In no time at all I was convinced that this was not a good idea, and back into the house Dad took me. Now whenever it's stormy, I load up the dogs and head for the ocean to walk on the beach."

Diana also recorded, "The tower at Point Arena was 115 feet tall and had 151 steps to the top. I would follow Dad up those stairs and watch him turn the light off in the morning and help him pull the curtain around the windows so the sun wouldn't shine on the prisms. In the evening, I would go up with him and reverse the process. On the weekends, visitors were allowed on the station and could go up the tower accompanied by a crew member. If it was my father who happened to be on watch, I'd be right behind everyone, and I'd be giving facts about the tower. I was probably accurate, as I'd heard Dad describe everything so often, but I'm sure some of the visitors thought I was a pest–and rightfully so!"

As with all lighthouse children, the Owens girls were expected to do their share of chores. When the twins were in the sixth or seventh grade, one of their chores before school was to turn off the light in the lighthouse tower. The light was electrified by this time and moved by a clockwork mechanism. Joan wrote in her journal, "We must have done a satisfactory job because we were soon asked if we would like to turn on the light in the evenings. It saved my dad from going up and down the stairs twice a day (he went up several times a day), and we always made a game of it. We always tried to run up all 141 steps, but I don't recall ever making it all the way without stopping and resting three quarters of the way up. Sometimes we went outside on the catwalk. One time I remember hanging on to the railing for dear life as the wind blew so hard–we felt like it was going to pick us up and carry us away. It was horrible, and when my father found out, he stressed the danger even for adults because of the wind. I can assure you, I never went outside on the catwalk again until I was older and only when the wind was calm."

Jean wrote, "The tower was a magnificent tall building with a spiral staircase inside. Many times while Joan and I were small, we would run up these stairs while Dad followed a bit slower. The metal stairs consisted of 144 steps with a landing every so often and a window. The fields, barns, and houses became miniatures the higher we climbed. It was exciting but frightening. As Joan and I got older Dad taught us how to light the tower. Our older sisters had already accomplished this feat. I think it was pretty clever of Dad to let us think it was an honor and privilege to do this very important task. I do know I loved having the responsibility, while it probably was quite tiring for Dad to go up and down the tower so often.

"Looking out the window from the very top," Jean continued, "would give anyone a thrill. I was able to see miles across the blue ocean. Our favorite beaches seemed to be only small strips of sand with pounding, frothy waves rolling over them. The fields were a hazy glow of yellows, blues, pinks, and lavenders as the wildflowers grew in wild abandonment. Far off in the distance I could see our cow, Bessie, and her new calf."

Joan told more about Bessie. "We had a cow to supply us with all the milk our family needed. Dad milked for a while but gave it up due to hay fever, so it soon became Mother's job. Mom would make cottage cheese, buttermilk, and butter. We all had to take turns churning the cream too—we would churn first with the left arm, then the right. It was always a challenge to see whether we would get butter first or have our arms drop off."

Bessie caused quite a scene on one occasion. Isabel detailed the story. "One morn-

ing I started for the barn to milk Bessie. She was nowhere in sight. It was raining, and I was getting soaked. Finally I decided I'd walk around the bluff to see if she had fallen off. As I walked behind the engine room I saw her standing on a ledge about seven feet from the top. I called to her to come up. She tried, but every time she put her hoof on the bank, it gave way. The soil was very soft from the rain, so I had to get help. The men rigged a block and tackle and planned to use the Packard to pull her up. Two men got down where she was and tied a rope around her, then they pushed as Bill started pulling with the car. When she was on top, she just walked away as though nothing had happened."

Another favorite family animal, a black dog named Pal, came to the girls one night when they were camping out in a tent near the lighthouse. Isabel tells about the man who came to claim the pup, but the girls had fallen in love with it and offered five dollars for him. The owner accepted. Jean furthered the story.

Looking much like General MacArthur, Keeper Owens stands watch atop Point Arena Lighthouse. *Bill Owens diligently kept his eyes on changes in the weather, ships passing too close to shore, and the whereabouts and doings of his six daughters. "Dad never had to say a thing to any one of us," youngest daughter Diana grins. "All he had to do was look at us!" Photograph courtesy of the Owens family*

"Pal was gentle and would go everywhere with Joan and me wherever we happened to be at the light station. He was very devoted to our family. Often he would run ahead of us, but never too far, as he would always run back to us as if to say, 'Why are you so slow? Hurry or you will miss all the excitement!'

"Across the open field behind the barn a strange little sticker grew in profusion amongst the strawberries. Somehow Pal always managed to cross the field with us through the stickers, but on the way home it was an entirely different story. All of a sudden he was unable to maneuver through the stickers. I do believe he was an old fake as he knew one of us would carry him home. This was no small feat as Pal was not exactly a small dog. But Pal was like a member of the family and you certainly would not leave a member of the family to suffer in a world of stickers.

"My sisters and I were playing on a gentle slope down over one of the cliffs. As this gentle slope continued for several yards it looked as though it would then continue on

Point Arena Light Station about 1940
The Owens girls spent hours exploring the cliffs leading down to the ocean. They had dozens of secret places where they played or retreated for some rare time alone. Photograph courtesy of the Owens family

around the curve forever. Pal was running, and as he started up the slope I knew immediately he was headed for the drop off. To this day I don't know if I tried to call him back or if I instinctively knew it was too late. He fell over the cliff to a beach that was many, many feet below. We quickly peered over the edge to see if he had fallen into the ocean but were tremendously relieved to see he had landed on the beach."

Jean continued the sad story. "There was absolutely no way for anyone to descend to Pal's aid. We quickly summoned Mom and Dad to help. We had no idea at the time that he had been badly injured. Due to the inaccessibility of the beach, my father backed the Packard toward the cliff and lowered one of the sailors stationed at the lighthouse on a rope tied to the bumper and backed the car closer to the edge. The sailor then trussed up Pal, and Dad drove forward until our dog was brought to the top. Dad repeated the process to retrieve the sailor. It was a dramatic time in our lives, but it also taught me a lesson that I still carry with me. 'Never assume or take things for granted.' Pal died not too long after the accident, and I've sorely missed our dear friend and companion ever since."

A keeper's wife is seldom given the recognition deserved for weathering many a rough time. Cooking, cleaning, raising children, serving as assistant or substitute keeper, and being a supportive wife were all part of the daily job. Isabel recorded a number of the behind-the-scenes stories of life at Point Arena. "While Bill was serving as an enlisted man in the coast guard reserve, it was required that he always wear a hat with his uniform when on duty. Often he went without the hat if the weather permitted. Two officers, on an inspection trip, reprimanded him for not having the hat on. A year after the war when he had returned to civilian status, the same officers arrived again. Bill happened to be wearing his hat until he recognized them driving in. Then he quickly took his hat off and threw it back in the house. As soon as the officers got out of their car one remarked to Bill, 'I told you to wear your hat when on duty.' Bill answered, 'I'm a civilian now, and it is not up to you to tell me what is required.'

"On another occasion two other officers arrived for inspection. First of all they noticed that the station truck did not have dust caps on the tires. Bill said they were lost. When the officers started for the fog signal to look over things, Bill told one of his men to take the dust caps off the officers' car, throw them away, and then get lost—go into town or someplace. Later, when they finished inspecting the fog signal and tower, the officers returned to their car. Bill looked at their car wheels and remarked that they did not have dust caps on their tires either. The officers looked at the wheels and remarked they must have lost them. I'm sure they realized what must have happened, but they did not say anymore about it!"

Joan wrote about surprise inspections. "There were times when my father would get a call early in the morning from the lifeboat station office to tell him the commanders were on their way over to the lighthouse for a surprise inspection. Mom would be in the middle of preparing breakfast and packing lunches, while some of us were getting dressed and others were waiting their turn to get into the bathroom. As soon as the news hit, we would all have to stop what we were doing. We'd make a mad dash to the bedroom to make the beds and straighten up, then run to the living and dining rooms to clean there. Poor Mom would frantically be trying to finish our lunches and clean the kitchen. What havoc those commanders caused by their little sneak inspection arrival! Most of the chores that hurriedly had to be done in five minutes would normally wait until Mom returned after taking us to school. We couldn't be late because she used our Packard for a bus to pick up other children on the other side of town. My mother should have received a commendation from the coast guard!"

As soon as the girls were old enough, they were given assigned chores. But they were fun, too, as Diana wrote. "The floors at the light station were covered with what is called battleship linoleum, a brown flooring, very hard to keep clean and shined. Since we were liable to have the quarters inspected at anytime, it was an ongoing battle. When Mom would wax the floor, she would fix up a pair of old pants with a pillow sewn in the seat. One of us would sit on the pillowed part, and a sister would grab the legs and slide the 'buffer' around the floor. We thought it was great fun, and Mom was getting the floor buffed in the process! If Mom had told us the purpose, I'm sure we wouldn't have decided it was fun after all."

All of the girls remembered Christmas as a special family time. Jean's journal tells,

Keeper Owens and Harry Danish, a friend from San Francisco, inside Point Arena Lighthouse
Keeper Owens kept watch duty in this room in the lighthouse tower. Photograph courtesy of the Owens family

"The best time of the year for me was Christmas at home by the ocean. We never had snow but always hoped it would rain. To this day I love rain, partly because it reminds me of Christmas and also because the outdoors take on such a fresh glistening glow.

"Several weeks before Christmas the whole family would load into the Packard and head for the mountains. There we would tramp through the woods looking for the perfect Christmas tree. The woods are a wonderful fairyland with the tall, majestic pines and the huckleberry and blueberry bushes. I wonder if Mom and Dad knew how much Joan and I loved the beauty of the woods? It was like being wrapped in a soft, green cocoon, and I would wonder, how did God make a place so beautiful to see and so wonderful to smell? I do believe that the odor of pine is the most glorious smell in the world.

"Our Christmas tree was always set in a prominent place in the large dining room," Jean wrote. "We all helped Mom unwrap the delicate Christmas balls that she had brought from Baltimore when she married in 1922. The last item to go onto the tree was the lead tinsel. It seemed to add the finishing touch that made our tree become magical. How I loved it all. The fireplace would be burning, and it would be warm and cozy as we all sat around the hearth and dreamed our dreams of presents.

"My sister Sarah would get up and exclaim that some homemade fudge would be the absolute perfect refreshment, while my sister Shirley would go with her to the kitchen to make popcorn. Later, while enjoying the fruits of Shirley's and Sarah's labors, we would listen to *Inner Sanctum.*"

As the girls grew up, their lighthouse family began to expand. Diana's journal revealed the fact that five of the girls married coastguardsmen. "Four of the guys arrived at Point Arena going with other girls–but they married Owens girls! I was different, I married a navy man. When we transferred to Point Cabrillo, Mom and I stopped at a store to pick up milk and bread. Joe Brown walked into the store–I had never seen him before in my life. I said, 'Mom, that's the boy I'm going to marry.' And I did!"

Diana summed up her feelings of her lighthouse days. "My memories bring many things to mind–the quiet and solitude I was allowed and the freedom to grow and explore. But my main memory is the beauty. The weather was usually windy or foggy, but that is beautiful in itself–those were the times I loved to be outside. We also had days when the ocean was so calm, with blue skies and sparkling water. And the most beautiful of all, the storms and being thankful you were inside a warm house with the family. The sound of a foghorn today brings a feeling of peace to me."

FAMILY RECIPES

Cora Isabel Owens baked many cakes in the Point Arena keeper's kitchen for her husband, her six daughters, and their friends.

APPLESAUCE CAKE

1½ cups brown sugar
1 unbeaten egg
1 square butter
1½ cups freshly made
hot applesauce
1 teaspoon baking soda

2½ cups flour
1 teaspoon cinnamon
1 teaspoon nutmeg
Raisins
Nuts

Blend all ingredients together. Line a loaf pan with waxed paper, and pour mixture into pan. Bake about 1 hour at 350° or until a toothpick comes out clean.

RHUBARB CRISP

Fresh rhubarb
½ to ¾ cup sugar
1 cup flour

⅓ cup butter
1 cup brown sugar
1 teaspoon baking powder

Cut rhubarb into small pieces and put into pie plate; sprinkle with sugar. Crumble together flour, butter, brown sugar, and baking powder. Sprinkle on top of rhubarb. Covered loosely with foil and bake at 375° for 20 minutes. Remove foil and continue baking for about 10 minutes or until fruit is tender.

When you visit Point Arena Light Station, picture a mother and daughter walking beneath the stars together under the sweep of the lighthouse beacon, twin girls running up the spiral staircase with their father in tow to turn on the light, and a family gathered around a bonfire on the beach. The Owens girls returned to Point Arena Lighthouse in 1995 to spread the ashes of their mother, Cora Isabel Owens. Their family bond remains as strong and dependable as the lighthouse beacon.

Keeper Owens at his retirement ceremony at Point Cabrillo Light Station, in California, in 1963

At his retirement ceremony, the coast guard honored Keeper William "Bill" Owens for his thirty-three years of dedicated service. Bill was the last civilian to serve at a West Coast lighthouse. Photograph courtesy of the Owens family

POINT ARENA LIGHT STATION is in the small town of Point Arena, about three and a half hours north of San Francisco on California Route 1. From San Francisco take U.S. Highway 101 north (inland) to Santa Rosa, turn west onto River Road, and continue to Route 1. Take Lighthouse Road north out of Point Arena to the light station.

The light station is open daily 10 a.m. to 4:30 p.m. from April until September and 11 a.m. to 2:30 p.m. the rest of the year. Docents greet visitors and provide information about the light station. Be sure to make the climb to the top of the tower to see the spectacular view of the surrounding mountains, ocean, and reefs.

There is an excellent museum and gift shop located in the old foghorn building. You also may want to stop at Rollerville Junction, about two miles from the lighthouse, which has unique crafts from the area and a large collection of lighthouse memorabilia.

For more information contact Point Arena Light Station at P.O. Box 11, Point Arena, CA 95468; 707/882-2777 or 877/725-4448.

CAPE HATTERAS
THROUGH THE EYES OF A KEEPER'S SON

Unaka Jennette, the last keeper of Cape Hatteras Lighthouse, was born in 1882 to Benjamin and Dorcas Jennette and began his career as a deckhand on the Diamond Shoals lightship in 1904. From 1911 to 1913 he served as captain of another lightship and a lighthouse tender before taking command of the Diamond Shoals relief lightship, which temporarily replaced the Thimble Shoals lightship and others that needed repairs or had been blown off station. In 1919 Captain Unaka won the highly prized principal keeper's position at Cape Hatteras and earned due respect for his distinguished service over the next twenty years. When a killer hurricane and devastating floodwaters assaulted Cape Hatteras Light Station in 1933, the Jennette family took refuge inland. Beach erosion threatened the lighthouse tower in 1936, and the light was moved to a steel tower in Buxton. Unaka spent his remaining U.S. Lighthouse Service years at the less important screwpile-style Roanoke Marshes Light, where he retired in 1943. Cape Hatteras Lighthouse remained darkened until 1950, and the Jennette family did not return to the keeper's house for almost thirty years.

Rany, the second son of seven children born to Unaka and Sudie Jennette, once served as a park ranger at the Cape Hatteras National Seashore. He enjoyed telling stories on the front porch of the Double Keepers' Quarters about growing up at the lighthouse. Only a few yards away stands his birthplace, the 1870 principal keeper's house, constructed of materials left over from the lighthouse tower built the same year. Rany shared his vivid memories of life at Cape Hatteras Light Station, as seen through the eyes of a keeper's son.

On a mild Sunday evening in 1928, about thirty minutes before dusk, visitors could stand on the north side of Cape Hatteras Lighthouse and look across several hundred feet of smooth beach to the Atlantic Ocean. They would see Principal Keeper Unaka Jennette walk out of the new screened porch on the east side of the keeper's house and adjust the lapels of his coat before he walked southward to the kerosene storage tank to fill his brass can. They would watch him ascend the first of the 268 steps of Cape Hatteras Lighthouse, and if they climbed the spiral staircase behind him, they would see him carefully fill the reservoir with kerosene and light the lamp inside the first-order

Standing on the running board of the Jennette family's Model T about 1925 are (from left) Vivian and Myrtle Casey, the assistant keeper's daughters, and Myrtle Jennette; Rany is standing inside the car and Mother Sudie is holding Olive.

Keeper Unaka Jennette used the family car to carry sick and injured islanders to the doctors in Elizabeth City. He also used it to haul fish for neighbors, a friendly gesture his wife, Sudie, did not wholeheartedly endorse. Photograph courtesy of the Jennette family

Keeper Unaka Jennette and the family Model T on board the primitive ferry from Hatteras Island to Bodie Island, the first leg of the journey to pick up the U.S. Lighthouse Service inspector in Norfolk, Virginia

It was a two-day inconvenience for Keeper Jennette to provide transportation for the inspector, but it thankfully cut down on the number of surprise inspections, something all lighthouse families dreaded. Photograph courtesy of the Jennette family

Rany and his younger sister Olive in the yard between their house and Cape Hatteras Lighthouse

The Jennettes and the children of the assistant keepers spent most of their free time either looking for "treasure" on the beach or playing croquet and other games in the yard at Cape Hatteras Light Station. "We were outside more than inside," Rany comments. "The keepers kept everything white-washed—even the cement-rein-forced fence posts and the rocks we kids brought back from the beach." Photograph courtesy of the Jennette family

Fresnel lens. The light would then begin its normal nocturnal rotation and continue its distinctive flashing until the keeper extinguished it after Monday's sunrise.

If the visitors peeked through the window of the porch door, they would see Captain 'Naka's logbook opened to that day's page on the keeper's rolltop desk and clothing that needed mending on the treadle sewing machine. They would also see the keeper's family and neighbors in the glow of the kerosene lamps in the dining room, which served as the family room. Almy, fifteen years old and dreaming of leaving the next year to join the navy, would be playing checkers with brother Rany, then seven years old. Sitting on the rug near the Victrola, five-year-old Olive would be playing with paper dolls cut from last year's Sears and Roebuck catalog. Twelve-year-old Vivian, nine-year-old Myrtle, and friends from Buxton would be gathered around the piano in the front room, while Mother Sudie, with one-year-old Dorcas on her lap, would be playing her favorite hymns and leading the Sunday night singing. Sudie would be expecting her seventh child, who would be named Ramona.

Providing for a family this size was a challenge, to say the least. But Cape Hatteras

Light Station provided all that was conducive not only to survival but also to a rather comfortable existence. Rany describes the vegetable garden his family grew to complement the canned foods they bought at a general store on their regular trek into Buxton. "We grew the usual–tomatoes, collards, cucumbers, beans. We went into town once a month. That was an exciting thing for us kids."

Now town wasn't far away as the crow flies. But road-wise, it was either take the beach "road," literally the sand beach trail, or the mud tracks into town. And it meant getting stuck in the mucky indentations of previous vehicles, climbing out of the car, putting planks down, and applying good old elbow grease to push the car to solid ground. Often the elbows became literally greased with the sandy Outer Banks mud that looked like tar. "On Sundays, by the time we reached the Methodist Church, our clothes looked pretty bad," Rany recalls.

Twelve-year-old Myrtle and ten-year-old Rany in their Sunday best

"Most people thought Myrtle and I were twins, we were so close," Rany says fondly of his older sister. "We were dressed up for church and happy about going into town and seeing other friends," he explains about this picture, taken about 1931. Photograph courtesy of the Jennette family

The Jennette children's backyard harbored merchant marine ships, freighters, side-paddle lighthouse tenders–vessels of every description. Lighthouse tenders periodically brought supplies that were checked on board by Keeper Jennette, lightered to shore by smaller boats, and picked up by horse-drawn carts at the landing. Mail was delivered from Manteo, usually every afternoon. News from the outside world arrived along with the new Sears and Roebuck catalog or a letter from a relative announcing a visit. Rany adds, "I remember some of the side-wheeler tenders. I believe they were the *Speedwell,* the *Mistletoe,* the *Holly,* and the *Violet.*"

The tenders, which hailed from Baltimore or Norfolk, supplied light stations all along the coast and tended the buoys as well. "Sometimes the district lighthouse inspector came along and did his inspection then. Everything had to be just right," Rany says.

Once in a while the lighthouse tenders would slip in through Pamlico Sound and anchor about 4 miles offshore in Cape Channel. "I loved it when a ship anchored near the lighthouse to do business with my father and the captain invited me to eat a meal with the crew," Rany smiles. Sometimes while Rany was on board he got to do something he often daydreamed about—explore the ship. His favorite part of any ship was the engine room, and Rany vowed to become an expert ship's machinist and travel the ocean's highways to new adventures.

Rany and the other keepers' children became extremely resourceful in creating playthings, and they took good care of everything they had. Rany remembers using lumber washed ashore to build a wagon and tearing tin cans in half to serve as fenders. He learned this efficiency from his father, who had to turn in old supplies before he could get new ones. For instance, to replace a worn, frazzled paintbrush, the keeper would have to send the proper requisition form to the U.S. Lighthouse Service and then surrender the old brush to the captain of the lighthouse tender, who meticulously checked off every item on the official supply list. Since supplies were delivered only once or

Nero, the Jennette family dog, appears to be surveying the floodwaters from a killer 1933 hurricane. *This photograph, taken from the lighthouse tower looking toward the principal keeper's house, shows the 1933 floodwaters that ruined the Jennettes' personal belongings and forced all of the keepers and their families to abandon Cape Hatteras Light Station. Rany remembers that "in back of the house, about 100 feet, were the pens where our cows, calves, and horses were kept. My mother and father always had a garden back there too." Photograph courtesy of the Jennette family*

Unaka Jennette, the last keeper of Cape Hatteras Lighthouse, polishing the prisms of the first-order Fresnel lens

Principal Keeper Jennette posed for National Geographic photographer Clifton Adams in 1933, and this picture appeared in the December issue. "A lot of time was spent polishing the lens," Rany notes. "Sometimes I helped him of course. My father was very particular about the upkeep of the station." Photograph by Clifton Adams, courtesy of the National Park Service

twice a year, the keeper had to make sure each wornout item was duly documented and carefully saved to be turned in to receive new ones.

Like all lighthouse children, Rany helped with the daily chores. He often climbed the tall tower to help his father "polish brass and polish brass and POLISH BRASS!" Rany loved to watch his father feed kerosene from the five-gallon brass can into the mantle lamp, trim the wick, clean the slender, graceful chimney glass, and polish the hundreds of prisms that formed the beehive-shaped lens.

Keeping every surface sparkling clean was top priority for everyone living at a light station, and the Jennettes along with every other keeper's family dreaded the official lighthouse inspectors' visits, especially surprise visits. The Jennettes endured fewer surprise visits than most lighthouse families, however, because Rany's father had to make a two-day trip that started with driving to Buxton to catch the ferry across Oregon Inlet and then driving all the way to Norfolk, Virginia, to pick up the inspector, a naval officer stationed in Washington, D.C.

One day, knowing the Cape Hatteras Light Station was due an inspection, Rany and one of his friends decided to help Keeper Jennette earn the revered "Inspector's Efficiency Star." Full of energy and good intentions, the boys found two paintbrushes,

dipped them into the vat of tar (which had been thinned by the summer heat to the consistency of paint) sitting alongside the granite steps at the base of the tower, and eagerly set about painting the tower's red base. Just as a beaming Rany was stepping back to look at the completed artwork, Keeper Jennette, whose protective feelings for the lighthouse were second only to those for his family, boomed, "Did you do this, Rany?"

"Yes, Sir!" Rany said with pride.

"I'm in a hurry to catch the last ferry to get the inspector and don't have time to deal with this now, but after the inspection is over we will talk about it."

Rany knew by the tone of his father's voice that there would be more than just a talk, and to add insult to injury, he would have to wait two or three days to find out just exactly what his father meant. The next few days seemed like an eternity for young Rany. "Guilty or not, I knew I was going to get it. I never knew my father to be angry, but I knew something was coming to me."

After Inspector "Captain" King's visit, Keeper Jennette picked up his leather razor strap, and Rany knew he did not intend to shave–his face, that is. Sixty years hence, the sting of that lesson endures, as does the indelible mark Rany left on the base of Cape Hatteras Lighthouse.

Captain 'Naka's strong hands meant both discipline and security to Rany. Even after so many years have passed, Rany recalls his father's strong hands carrying him up to the lantern room of Cape Hatteras Lighthouse for the first time. He still feels those strong hands reaching over the side railing of a large tender ship to lift him to safety when he almost fell out of a smaller boat. And he still sees those strong hands gently remove his sister's head from the smallest of the three holes in their first-class privy when it got stuck while she was watching Rany hook turtles through the largest hole. "I was real nervous when I looked over and saw no head on Ramona. I ran for my father,"

Rany tells in his quiet manner.

When Rany got old enough, he helped round up and mark the wild ponies on Hatteras Island. Every man on the island knew who owned a pony by the brand on its rump. The Jennette brand was a "J."

Most of the animals on Hatteras Island ran loose until a law was passed against it. "The first time I ever knew my father to show his temper was when state men came and claimed a cow and her calf after that law was passed. He looked and looked for them. When he got back to the pen, a state horseman had them there, ready to take them. 'I'll take my cow and calf,' my father told the man. 'They don't belong to you anymore; they're the state's now,' the man told my father. Well he rode home, got his gun, went back to the pen area, and shot both the cow and calf. 'Now you can take them,' my father told the state man.

Unaka Jennette was known as a fair man and helpful in time of need. He had one of the few cars on Hatteras Island and provided an "ambulance service" for anyone who needed to be taken to doctors in Elizabeth City. Keeper Jennette transported more than people in the family car, however. "If someone got a big haul of fish and needed to get it out to market, my father would help with our car. One time he took out the back seat of our brand new Model T, loaded the smelly fish, and hauled it to be put on ice. Now my mother, Sudie, didn't think much of him getting stinking fish in our new car!"

Keeper Jennette expected his children to be useful in every way they could. The girls helped with the housework and cleaning, a tremendous job for a keeper's wife with seven children. Fortunately Sudie had a gasoline-powered washing machine to help keep up with the endless loads of family laundry. Most of the time Sudie and the girls cooked on a wood or coal stove in the house, but to minimize the oppressive heat in the summer, they used a three-burner kerosene stove in the detached kitchen. An oak icebox on the side porch kept perishables cool.

The boys helped with the pigs, chickens, cows, ponies, and vegetable garden. "But life was good," Rany quickly adds. "I grew up with a brother and five sisters, the two assistant keepers' families, and the surfmen and their families from nearby Cape Hatteras Life-saving Station. While we lived at Cape Hatteras Light Station, eight assistants' families lived there. They were usually big families, too, with lots of kids. Three I can quickly recall were the Cayce, Quidley, and Fulcher families. There was always somebody visiting and very competitive games of croquet going on. It wasn't a lonely life like most think," Rany finishes.

Until 1905 three assistant keepers served at Cape Hatteras Light Station. The main duty of the third assistant was to take care of Cape Hatteras Beacon, which had been erected in 1856 about a mile and a half southwest of the main Hatteras tower. The

23-foot-tall beacon had a square white (at one time recorded "red") tower with a black lantern canopy and brown piles and roof. It displayed a fixed white light from a sixth-order Fresnel lens, so rare today that it is called the "gem." Positioned on the tip of Cape Point, then known as the "Bight," Cape Hatteras Beacon served coasting (local) boaters cutting through the slough channel to Hatteras Inlet and Pamlico Sound. It survived until 1906 when it succumbed to a devastating combination of wind and storm waves. The beacon disappeared from the official list of beacons, buoys, and day-marks in the fifth lighthouse district, and the third assistant keeper was out of a job.

The two remaining assistant keepers and their families continued to live and work alongside the Jennettes at Cape Hatteras Light Station until beach erosion forced the U.S. Lighthouse Service to darken the lighthouse in 1936. Electricity and indoor plumbing did not come to the Cape Hatteras keepers' dwellings until four years after the families had left. These modern conveniences were provided for the groups of Civilian Conservation Corps who had come to Hatteras Island to build the controversial dune system on the Outer Banks. Rany believes that erosion would not be a problem at Cape Hatteras if nature were allowed to sculpt the land as it was meant to do, but natural overwash is too much a bother in modern times, especially with businesses sitting on the edge of hard-surfaced roads.

"We didn't miss electricity or plumbing," Rany says frankly. "As long as the Hatteras light worked, that's what mattered." When asked about the distinctive characteristics of the light that flashed from Cape Hatteras Lighthouse tower, Rany responds without thinking, "One and a half seconds on and six seconds eclipse. I saw that flash every night through my bedroom window. It put me to sleep."

One big occasion at the lighthouse that Rany particularly remembers is when his sister Vivian became engaged in 1935. Her future groom, Shelley Frontis, ran up the steps of the tallest brick lighthouse in the world to ask Keeper Jennette for his daughter's hand in marriage. Rany smiles when he pictures his father busily cleaning the 7-foot mass of prisms with rouge polish while listening to a panting, excited young man who wanted to become a son-in-law. "I remember when Vivian got married in the Methodist parsonage in Buxton and when she left," Rany says quietly. Like many children who grew up in lighthouses, both Rany and his sister still live near their childhood home.

Mention "hurricane" and Rany reacts with the same indifference he would if you had just mentioned rain. "When you grow up with storms, it's just a normal event," he explains. "Hurricanes and bristling nor'easters scare the devil out of city dwellers, but for islanders, it's nature's way of claiming her freedom to do her work; master cleaning, if you will," he adds.

The first hurricane of 1933 brought high seas and winds over eighty miles per hour

The Jennette family in front of the principal keeper's house in 1962

The Jennette family gathered at the Cape Hatteras principal keeper's house in 1962 to celebrate Unaka's eightieth birthday. It marked the first time they had returned to the light station since hurricane beach erosion had forced them to abandon the lighthouse in 1936. Mother Sudie had always wanted to go back to her home of twenty years, but she passed away in 1960 and could be with them only in spirit. The National Park Service added house numbers when it took the light station under its care; it is now restoring the keeper's house to its 1930's appearance, when Rany and his family called it "home." Photograph courtesy of the Jennette family

to Cape Hatteras. With no man-made dune system in place, the normal flooding was experienced with the usual cleanup afterward. Rany loved strong storms like that one once in a while because it meant playing pirates on the beach with wonderful treasures to claim. He found shells of every shape and color. Driftwood stirred his imagination and became all sorts of animals. Even "gold" washed up from ships caught in the hurricane's blow. Rany remembers riding his favorite pony, Wildfire, with abandonment to "exotic places decorated with sand castles and washed by emerald waves."

The second hurricane of 1933, however, threatened Cape Hatteras with higher seas and stronger winds. Even while it was still approaching the Outer Banks, Captain 'Naka knew that storm would be a killer. He and the assistant keepers sent their families inland for safety while they stationed themselves in the lighthouse tower to ride out the hurricane's fury. "A keeper was never to leave his station, no matter what," Rany comments on his father's duties. After the wind and rain subsided, Keeper Jennette opened the door of the lighthouse to find the ocean lapping against the tower and the compound completely flooded.

The Jennette family's temporary move inland became permanent. The tide had swept through their beautifully furnished home at the light station, ruining the oak dining table, couches, the keeper's desk, and the many items bought from salvage auctions after shipwrecks on the Outer Banks. Everything in the house but a few brass lamps and a spittoon with U.S.L.H.S. stamped on it belonged to the Jennettes, and they suffered great personal loss.

Beach erosion seriously threatened the safety of the tower in 1936, and the U.S. Lighthouse Service decided to darken Cape Hatteras Lighthouse and move the light to a steel structure in Buxton. Keeper Jennette took on the duty of manning the cold, skeletal tower that held a modern lighting device—quite a change from the proud, solid brick tower and its kerosene lamp. The Jennette family would not return to Cape Hatteras Light Station until 1962, when they celebrated Unaka's eightieth birthday.

During the lighthouse's eclipse from 1936 until it was recommissioned in 1950, vandals damaged the historic Cape Hatteras tower and its magnificent Fresnel lens. Eventually some unknown person or persons took what was left of the lens, and its location remains an unsolved mystery, although every once in a while a prism or section of the lens is found or surrendered.

After high school, Rany worked for a while and then enlisted in the coast guard and joined the crew of the cutter *Hamilton* in June 1941. In January 1942 the coast guard sent Rany to a training school in New York, which—fortunately—forced him to miss out on a subchaser cruise. On January 29, 1942, the *Hamilton* was torpedoed off the coast of Iceland. Of the twenty-seven crewmen killed, nineteen were in the engine room, exactly where Rany would have been had he been on board. Another lighthouse keeper's son, Carl Jaehne, who had grown up in California's Pigeon Point Lighthouse (see page 116), was on board the *Hamilton* and—also fortunately—survived the torpedo attack.

From January through March 1942 American navy and coast guard ships played a deadly game of hare and hound with German U-boats along the eastern seaboard of the United States. Just offshore from Rany's childhood home at Cape Hatteras Light Station, the Germans sank at least one American ship a day during that period. Tankers made prime targets, and most of the oil coming from Texas and the Caribbean spilled into the ocean off the Carolina coast. With other valuable cargo as well as priceless lives being lost and the American war effort to protect her own shores and supply European allies in grave jeopardy, American crews turned their full attention to hunting U-boats. Rany joined in the hunt and rose to the rank of chief petty officer on submarine chaser 83328 running a hundred miles off the Virginia coast to protect Chesapeake Bay. He later joined the action off North Africa, doing convoy duty on the destroyer escort *Lansing* from 1943 until 1944.

After the war Rany traveled the world, unaware that he was really working his way back home. In 1970 he returned to Buxton, North Carolina, to manage the Cape Hatteras water system. In 1984 he joined the National Park Service as a seasonal staff member. He's a natural as an interpreter at the visitors center in Buxton, telling thousands of people every year about Cape Hatteras Light Station. In 1995 Rany met and married lighthouse volunteer Lynn O'Neill. They exchanged their wedding vows beside his boyhood home, with Cape Hatteras Lighthouse towering in the background.

"During my work history, I've worn with pride six different uniforms for the United States government. However none have I worn so proudly as the green and gray of the National Park Service," Rany says. Leaning against the railing of the double keepers' house, he shares his true-life stories. He tells of witnessing the development of the telephone and the automation of lighthouses that now stand alone. He speaks to today's youth about times when surviving the tricky Diamond Shoals depended on a working beacon light and when the survival of a family was based on working together. He tells of recent Hurricane Emily's namesake, a half-drowned kitten that bumped his boot when he opened the front door of his flooded house—and how Emily has learned to pull the rope to the bell at the front door when she is hungry.

Rany's memories help bring one person after another closer to understanding what working wonders lighthouses are. Visitors see the bricks and mortar, but even better, through Rany's eyes they see what daily life at Cape Hatteras Lighthouse was like.

There is no denying that when the big light comes on it is magic. As Rany says, "Come, if you can, and see."

FAMILY RECIPES

Hatteras Island foods have unique characteristics. Rany and his sisters describe their childhood diet as consisting mainly of "stews" made from chicken, pork, or fish. When they mention "dumplings," they are referring to a ½-inch or thinner, flat square made from cornmeal and put into the pot with other foods while they cooked to absorb the flavor of the main dish. "Pastry" was a flour-and-water dough rolled into thin pasta-style strips. The Jennette children also remember eating lots of "Mama's cakes."

Rany's wife, Lynn, pulled the following recipes from Mrs. Jennette's old recipe book that was used for many years at Cape Hatteras Light Station. With visitors always coming to visit the famous lighthouse and with the assistant keepers' families, the Cape Hatteras Life-saving Station crew and friends, and neighbors constantly dropping in, Mrs. Jennette baked her pineapple and prune cakes "about as many times as there are bricks in the lighthouse," according to Rany.

BOILED DRUM WITH CRACKLIN'

1 whole fish (cleaned and filleted)
3 large potatoes (or more if desired)
2 medium onions (or as desired)
1 piece about 1 inch thick by 7 inches long of salt pork (diced)
1 onion, sliced for serving with cooked fish

Peel potatoes and onions and cut into quarters. Cut fish into serving pieces.
Put fish, potatoes, and onions into pot and boil until done.
Fry the diced salt pork until crispy.
When fish and potatoes and onions are cooked, arrange on platter and pour
cracklin' (salt pork) over everything. Serve with sliced raw onions.

COLLARDS AND CORNMEAL DUMPLINGS

Clean and devein collards and place in large pot with several pieces of salt
pork. Cook for several hours.

Dumplings:
1 cup cornmeal   ½ teaspoon salt
⅓ cup flour

Mix together and scald with boiling water. Form into flat patty-shaped
dumplings. Place dumplings into boiling collard pot (lining the sides of pot)
until the dumplings are just covered with liquid. Cook 45 minutes to an
hour.

PONE BREAD ("MOM'S BREAD")

2 cups cornmeal   1 tablespoon molasses
½ cup flour   5 tablespoons sugar
4 tablespoons vinegar   1 teaspoon baking powder

Scald the meal and add the flour and thin; add the other ingredients. Leave
on the porch overnight. Bake in a liberal amount of shortening.

PRUNE CAKE WITH FROSTING

Cake:

3/4 cup shortening	1 teaspoon cinnamon
1 cup sugar	1 teaspoon nutmeg
3 eggs	1 teaspoon soda
2 cups flour	3 tablespoons sour cream
1 cup prunes	1/2 teaspoon salt

Note: Mrs. Jennette did not have any written directions for mixing and baking the cake.

Frosting:

1 cup sugar	1 cup sour milk
1 cup prunes	1 teaspoon vanilla
3 tablespoons butter	1 cup nuts
2 eggs	

Mix all ingredients together in saucepan and cook until thickened.

PINEAPPLE CAKE

Mix batter and bake a 2-layer yellow cake.

Pineapple Filling:

1 can crushed pineapple	Juice of 1 lemon
1 tablespoon sugar	

Boil pineapple, sugar, and lemon juice; thicken with some of the cake batter. Spread the pineapple filling over each cake layer.

Icing:

Powdered sugar	Canned milk
Butter	

Cream together all of the ingredients. Ice cake.

CAPE HATTERAS LIGHT STATION, part of Cape Hatteras National Seashore, is in Buxton, North Carolina, on Highway 12. The clearly marked road leading to the large visitors parking lot is on the ocean side of the highway.

The National Park Visitors Center is adjacent to the lighthouse and houses a bookstore/gift shop. The Double Keepers' Quarters is a museum that features exhibits about the "Graveyard of the Atlantic" and the Cape Hatteras Light Station. Also on display is the gold life-saving medal awarded to U.S. Life-Saving Service Keeper Benjamin Dailey for his daring efforts to rescue people on board the shipwrecked Ephraim Williams on Christmas 1884. The Principal Keeper's Quarters, Rany Jennette's birthplace, has been restored to its 1930s' appearance. The lighthouse, oil house, and both Keepers' Quarters were relocated in 1999 a safe distance from the ocean. Each part of the light station was carefully placed in its same historic position. For information on Cape Hatteras and interpretive programs, call a ranger at the visitors center desk at 252/475-9601.

Visitors may climb the spiral staircase to the top of Cape Hatteras Lighthouse any day from early April until mid-October weather permitting. For information about touring Cape Hatteras Light Station and interpretive programs, call the National Park Service Visitors Center at 252/473-2111.

PASSAGE ISLAND

TIMELESS PASSAGE

While working on freighters plying the Great Lakes when he was a young man, Vern Bowen learned to refer to lighthouses as "ladies." His respect for the proud towers and faithful beacons led him to pursue a career with the U.S. Lighthouse Service. Keeper Bowen served as first assistant keeper at Passage Island Light Station from 1930 to 1943, when he was transferred to New Presque Isle Light Station. Living and working alongside him during his many years of faithful lighthouse service were his wife, Cordelia "Billie" Mink, daughters Johanna and Anna, and son Vern, who was nicknamed "Sonny."

Anna Bowen Hoge (pronounced HO-gee) recalls her childhood on Passage Island far out in Lake Superior, the largest single freshwater lake in the world, large enough to have tides and very temperamental moods. More than four decades later, Anna still feels deeply connected to her childhood, a magical time on an island paradise filled with rare flora and fascinating fauna. Several years ago Anna decided to go back to the island and find out if the magic of her childhood is real or just part of her imagination. Feeling both trepidation and exhilaration, she stepped off a boat onto Passage Island for the first time in forty-two years and once again became ten-year-old Annie. She unearthed the treasure she had buried as an offering to the island when she "abandoned" it, and she reclaimed the warmth of her family. Anna joyfully recalls her life as a keeper's daughter on Passage Island.

While German troops were invading Paris, Carl Sandburg was winning the Pulitzer prize for *Abraham Lincoln: The War Years*, Howard Florey was developing penicillin, scientists were taking their first look through an electron microscope, and "When You Wish upon a Star" was filling the airwaves, young Anna "Annie" Bowen was lying contentedly on her favorite rock on Passage Island high above the clear, cold waters of Lake Superior. She daydreamed in this spot, flat on her belly, chin cupped in hand. From here she could see all of the world before her, and she imagined herself a princess, her family being the richest people in the world with their fine island and their castle of a lighthouse.

Anna and her family lived at the light station from May through December and

Passage Island Light Station about 1900

Passage Island rises out of Lake Superior off the northeastern tip of Isle Royale, more than 60 miles from Houghton on the Michigan mainland. Passage Island Lighthouse, the northernmost light on the American side of the Great Lakes, has guided ships into Thunder Bay since 1882. Anna Bowen Hoge speaks of this lighthouse as her treasured home. She says, "I feel as if I lived during the most important times considering the knowledge, skill, and manpower it took to coordinate the U.S. Lighthouse Service before automation. Shipping was vital to all parts of the United States, with lumber going one way and finished products going the other. And it was my family's job to see that the ships passed safely." Photograph courtesy of Anna Bowen Hoge

moved to the Michigan mainland when ice on the Lake Superior curtailed shipping. "I remember living on Passage Island from the time my first memories formed," says Anna, who spent most of the first ten years of her life at this remote lighthouse outpost.

Anna's emotions serve as bookends holding the volumes of her memories. Occasionally she takes down a volume, opens it, and randomly turns back to the late 1930s and early '40s when she was a young child full of wonder, taking in every sight, sound, and smell. Thumbing through these memories, she can clearly see her father, her mother, her younger sister, Johanna, and her baby brother, "Little" Vern, known to the family as "Sonny." Anna can, at will, become young Annie on Passage Island.

Among Anna's poignant stories are some side-splitting Laurel-and-Hardy scenes, like this one about a memorable washday. "The United States Lighthouse Service issued big, heavy wool blankets," Anna begins. "My mom would wait for a special day to wash these blankets, a day that was just right on Passage Island. Though we kids never paid any attention, it was always cold and windy. Mother would hang these prized blankets, the only real security we had that we would be warm, on the clothesline outside our back door after washing them. My little brother had a strap harness, and he was tied to the clothesline. This way, we knew he wouldn't blow off the island in a storm that often came upon us quicker than you can ever imagine. One 'perfect' washday, Mom had the freshly laundered blankets on the line and my dad and Mr. Lane, the other keeper, were up in the tower working when one of those dreaded, sudden storms came charging in from the northwest. She rolled in real fast.

"The blankets were one moment peacefully hanging in the warm, glorious sun, and the next moment they were flying off the lines. In the event of an emergency, my sister's duty was to lie on top of little Sonny so he wouldn't blow away. He was hooked up to the line, but she still was to get on top of him and make sure he didn't end up in the lake. I remember the strong wind and those big blankets sailing out across Lake Superior–they looked like flying carpets!

"Dad came running down and caught one or two on the rocks before the lake swallowed them up, because when they hit the water, they sank. Mom was so upset seeing her clean blankets headed toward the mainland. These coverings were considered gold in the frigid climate of Passage Island, and there I was–so delighted to see this beautiful sight of magic carpets sailing out across the crystal blue water. But we lost our supply of warm blankets and had to wait for the next boat to come in and take a new requisition for more blankets. Until they arrived, we piled our winter clothes on top of our beds and wore caps and gloves to bed."

Anna continues her heartfelt monologue. "On the island there was no church, but we used the Holy Bible. If you didn't believe God was there, all you had to do was step outside, sit on the rocks, and look at the beauty. We were very much in a cathedral; we spent quality, loving time with our parents. The entire family loved to sit together on the bench my father had made among the birch trees. We kids would take turns on the swing Dad made, sometimes piling on top of one another and wildly swinging, trying to knock each other off. What fun it was to swing W-A-Y up and feel as if we were flying out over Lake Superior, like the graceful, hovering birds we watched with envy.

"We proudly looked at the small garden just in front of the foghorn building, which grew the beautiful flowers that made Mother feel like she lived in a civilized place and the cherished rhubarb from which Mother made pies and jams. People from Isle Royale would buy it from us because it couldn't be raised on the neighboring island. None of us kids would ever trade this time in our lives for anything else in the world. Our parents loved us, no matter what.

"My mother told a story many times about something I did. Right up until the day she died in 1987, she said she could have wrung my neck for this. Our gasoline supply was brought in by boat, and during the war years, this supply of gasoline was especially precious. It was brought in barrels by the lighthouse tender, and on one side of the island, workers would bury these barrels down in the ground after a tedious ride on the tram up the ramp. A spigot was put up so the keepers could draw out the gasoline and carry it in cans for its use in the lantern and foghorn engine. The gasoline was such a valuable commodity that a tuna can was carefully hung by a wire under the spigot so that even the last drops could be collected and used.

"As a child," Anna continues, "I loved the smell of gasoline; I still love the smell. We were told this area of the island was strictly forbidden—off limits for us kids. There were several areas we were to stay away from, but this one meant certain death if we violated what our parents ordered! Even though the barrels were buried safely many feet below the ground, it still was forbidden as a play area, and we kids knew very well that we were to stay away. It wasn't too far from the house. My mother would ring the big bell out in the yard for us, and we better be within answering distance by the tenth ring of the bell. Well the gasoline storage area was within the respected distance. We were playing with sticks, and we got to building a small fire. We would bring a small amount of the fuel from the barrel's spigot to our fire, and we were dripping a bit of it each time we hurriedly carried the gasoline from the spigot to the fire.

"Pretty soon we had a trail going from our fire, which we were building in a pretend game. We were imagining a life-threatening situation and our fire was the only thing that could save our frozen little lives. Meanwhile we did have a real problem on our hands—our little innocent fire for our pretend play lit the trail over to the spigot to the first barrel, and before we knew it, KABLOOEY! When she went up, we kids ran as we never had before! The first thing we did was to sit on my brother so he wouldn't get blown up. Then we watched in amazement as each barrel underground became part of the chain reaction—BOOM! BOOM! BOOM! It was no doubt the most beautiful Fourth of July you ever saw! Just beautiful!

"My mother came out screaming that the Japanese were bombing Passage Island. Her two brothers had been at Pearl Harbor when it was bombed, and she had just been waiting for the Japanese to sneak up on us. She thought our world as we knew it was coming to an end! My dad came over to us. We sat there on our brother, trying to appear responsible young people, certainly not the knotheads who had caused this.

Lighthouse tender ship *Marigold*

Tender ships served as lifelines for many lighthouse families, including the Bowens, who lived on isolated Passage Island, a good day's trip from the Michigan mainland. The tenders brought mail, books, food, and maintenance supplies. At least once a year the lighthouse inspector rode along to do his "white-glove" inspection of the light station. Photograph courtesy of Anna Bowen Hoge

"Dad remained calm, using the psychology that if he didn't get too upset with us, we would tell the truth. He said, 'Now, you've got to tell me what happened.' Since my clothes still smelled of gasoline, he had a pretty good idea who to ask. But for some reason, I couldn't muster the courage to speak at that moment. It dawned on me that I could just go jump off the steep cliff side of the island and probably satisfy everyone.

"We had to radio for more gasoline, plus Dad had to write a report as to why his supply was down. Petroleum, in any form during wartime, was rationed very carefully. I was very worried for my dad and the report he had to make; I knew there would be negative remarks from the lighthouse inspector who demanded perfection in record keeping. Sometime later I went to Dad and tried to talk, and all he could say was, 'We'll talk about this later.' I felt awful–except that I have a visual memory of those magnificent celebration-type fireballs going up in the sky!

"Annie," as she was known to her family, on Keeper Vern Bowen's knee, about 1937

"The years on Passage Island were the happiest I have ever known," says Anna. "My dad died when I was just starting out in life on my own, and I have always missed him dearly. He wanted to go back to Passage Island but never made it. When I go back, I look for him—and I see him in the beauty of the trees and flowers and ferns." Photograph courtesy of Anna Bowen Hoge

"When the boat came with a new supply of petroleum, the inspector was aboard. The keepers were called on the carpet to explain just what had happened. "My father had demanded that I be well dressed and available to talk with the inspector. 'You have to tell him,' my father told me. I told the inspector that it was all my fault. I knew my father would receive demerit points because of my careless child's play. So I told the inspector with as much respect as possible that Dad had many times told us kids not to go in that area, but that I loved the smell of gasoline so much, I just had to do what I did. I certainly had not planned to blow up the entire island.

"By the time the inspector had finished talking to us, we would never forget what he emphasized. He told us ships could go down, airplanes could crash, men could die, and all because I had to smell the gasoline, and somewhere, someone would not have enough fuel because of my immature desire. Boy, did I ever feel responsible. It was definitely the most awful feeling I had ever had. As kids, we knew our father's job was very important. We knew we were responsible for people and freight on ships, and for the first time, we got a picture of our part in it all."

From then on, respect for the lighthouse took precedence. "I knew my dad worked so hard in keeping the brass polished, the precious prisms of the small lens perfect with a special cloth, and the gasoline carefully measured and ready for the next night's work. He had always worked very hard—first as a young man on the freighters steaming their way through the Great Lakes."

While working on the freighters, Vern Bowen grew to depend on the network of lighthouses on the lakes, and he learned to refer to them respectfully as "ladies." This made it natural for the young man to pursue a career with the U.S. Lighthouse Service. "And here I was, Vern Bowen's daughter, undermining everything my father stood for," laments Anna. "So I felt I had to figure out a way to repent my great blunder. My sister helped me make salt and flour decorations and dry them on the radiators for the lonely servicemen overseas. I don't know where my father sent the things, but he did respect the fact that we were trying to make up for the gasoline we had blown up.

"The inspector came unannounced and at irregular intervals. If other lighthouses could, they would send some sort of warning so all could be gotten in shipshape. As a representative of the United States government, he would give everything the white-glove test—everything. He would even check the cookstove for hidden dirty dishes.

"One time when the inspector tried to make a surprise visit, Dad was up in the tower with his apron on, polishing the globe of the lantern. He decided to take a much-deserved break and stepped out on the catwalk to survey the lake and passing freighters. He focused his telescope on what appeared to be a small craft approaching Passage Island. He quickly identified the government boat and the stiff outline of the lighthouse inspector. What the inspector would find, my father always determined, was everything in its place.

"The boat docked at the bottom of the descent from the rocks at the landing on the leeward side of the island. Landing a boat was always precarious because of the strong currents and winds of Lake Superior. The inspector debarked the United States Lighthouse Service boat [this was prior to the merger with the coast guard in 1939] and walked confidently up the 130-or-so-foot tram to the back area of our house. He stopped to look up at the lighthouse tower and lantern that rose forty feet upward from the northwest corner of our house and which was connected to the foghorn building. Sonny had been untied from the clothesline just to the inspector's left as he passed the tram storage building. "We children hurriedly dressed in our best clothes as the men scrambled to get into their uniforms. They looked professional in their dark wool suits and the classy black-brimmed hats with the gold lighthouse emblem. But working in these itchy, confining outfits while doing the dirty jobs that came with being lighthouse employees just wasn't practical—paint on a uniform would mean certain negative marks.

"Well I had considered those unfair bad marks that could come with just a bit of dust on one of the lens's prisms. I decided it was time to take matters into my own competent hands. As we children sat dutifully mute on the steps to the kitchen while the inspector made his revered appearance, I made my move. The guest of honor passed by me, and I innocently reached up and took his hand. He stopped and looked back at me with one foot on my level and the other on the step below. My heart also stopped. I asked him to sit down beside me. He did. A large hush could be heard all over the island. My mother and father looked on with horror. 'What is Annie going to say?!' I could interpret from their expressions. I winked to reassure them—they would be so proud of me later.

"Mr. Inspector, I want to show you some things that are very RIGHT with our lighthouse and island. You should concentrate on the GOOD things instead of the old BAD!

" 'NO! Annie,' " my parents said in unison, trying to smile and hide their anxiety.

" 'No, Mr. and Mrs. Bowen, let Annie speak. Yes, dear, what is it you want to show me?'

"I began by showing the inspector the clean, rocky area surrounding the lighthouse that reached back toward the arboreal forest completing the island area. Next I showed him the freshly painted trim on the house, foghorn building, tram building, oil-storage building, and tower top. Then I led him up the steps to the all important beacon with its shining brass clockwork mechanism and oilcans. He pretended to be impressed with the sparkling glass of the storm panes and the gleaming prisms as they cast their spectrums upon the lantern room.

"Satisfied that I had ensured my father's present and future excellent ratings, I returned to my quiet place on the steps below in the kitchen while the inspector finished his visit with the men. The only thing I noticed while I gloated in my moment of glory was that mother looked a bit pale.

"After the inspector had left, my mother and father banned me to my room forever. They expected to receive a message at any moment to pack all our belongings and return to civil life.

"Well, fortunately, the inspector had a better sense of humor than they ever expected of him. Though my father did receive a reprimand, we were allowed to continue our stay. You can bet I learned well the lesson to stay out of adult business after that!"

Several months later the keeper's wife invited her nephew to visit them on the island. The boy usually stayed with his grandparents during the summer because they considered Passage Island too isolated for him, but this summer they allowed him to stay for several days. Anna and Johanna had found a seagull's nest on the cliffside of the island and had been eyeing it longingly for quite a while. Being adventurous, they made plans to get that bird and the nest of eggs, but neither had the nerve to actually go down the cliff to get them. "Newcomer, Larry Lane, became our nominee for most likely to succeed at being lowered by rope to retrieve the treasure," Anna recalls.

"My sister and I tied the rope around unsuspecting Larry and proceeded to lower him over the towering cliff. But we had one problem—although we could lower him by the rope, we weren't strong enough to pull him back up. We had him right by the nest, and he busied himself with the fascinating new discovery of the bird and its nest. We

Annie's brother, little Vern "Sonny," sitting with Mother Cordelia "Billie" Mink Bowen

Little Vern, nicknamed "Sonny," survived many "sittings" by his sisters. Since a sudden gust was capable of sweeping a small child right off the island, Sonny was placed in a harness tethered to the clothesline and as an added safety measure, older sister Johanna was responsible for "sitting" on him whenever the wind picked up. Both Johanna and Annie took to "sitting" on Sonny at other times too, especially when something exciting or dangerous happened. The youngster was sat on so many times that the family joked about Sonny having been "hatched." Photograph courtesy of Anna Bowen Hoge

actually got him back up to the top of the dangerous cliff and had him over the edge. But he was hanging onto the prized nest of eggs, so he couldn't–no, he wouldn't let go of them to help pull himself back up away from the long drop into Lake Superior.

"I held onto the rope tied to our trusting friend for dear life, and my sister held onto me for dear life. I watched as Larry's head sank below the cliff's horizon, then his shirt disappeared, then his upper leg, and finally his sneakers once again faded over the cliff's edge. Larry was screaming, I was screaming, and my sister was screaming! My sister let go of me, and Larry slipped farther toward the sharp rocks below. 'I've got you–don't worry!' I yelled to Larry, all the time sounding much more assured than I really was. Meanwhile, my sister ran for help.

"My dad and Mr. Lane came running as fast as they could when they realized my crazed sister was trying to tell them someone was dangling over the cliff's edge. They grabbed the rope and with two men's strength tried to pull poor Larry back to safety. When I realized I may have killed our only visitor, I started to question our choice of activities for that afternoon."

When Mr. Lane finally acknowledged that Larry was not going to return to the island's surface the way he had left, as the load for the human crane proved too much for even the men's strength, he ran to the boathouse, put the rowboat into the water, and proceeded toward his nephew for a daring rescue. Knowing how his parents overprotected him, Mr. Lane could imagine the wrath he would surely endure, not to mention that he would never see his nephew again—and his wife would surely have a few choice opinions of this situation.

"By the time Mr. Lane got to the cliff side where Larry hung like a wildly swinging pendulum, EVERYONE knew of our plight," Anna says with large hand gestures. "And EVERYONE was upset. My father held onto that rope like it was his last chance on earth for peace, and I was screaming at Larry to try to climb up the rocks, and my sister was dutifully sitting on my brother, as if something else went wrong we would all surely die for our sins in killing Larry. The way events were unfolding, it looked as if we were going to be successful in actually killing someone this time."

Keeper Lane called over the roar of the incoming Superior tide for Keeper Bowen to slowly lower Larry down to his awaiting boat. "Finally Mr. Lane safely had Larry in hand—and we all realized why the task had been so difficult: Larry was still hanging onto that blasted bird's nest and eggs! He wasn't about to let this entire effort be for naught. Well my sister and I got a spanking, and Larry got shipped back to his parents on the next boat to the mainland. That was the last time we saw Larry.

"Since our entertainment was limited, we were kids trying to make up our own fun. I remember when big fish were caught, we got the bladder to blow up like a ball. I must say, we learned to entertain ourselves! Sometimes we just didn't know how it would turn out!

"The only milk we had was the 'tin

Baby Vern on the lighthouse boat
"My baby brother, Vern, is standing on Dad's lighthouse service boat in this picture," says Anna. "This boat was our only means of transportation to Isle Royale, where we could catch the ferry that took us to the mainland, five more hours away." Photograph courtesy of Anna Bowen Hoge

(From left) Annie (wearing hat), Sonny, Larry Lane petting Spot, and Larry's cousin, about 1939

Larry's curiosity and determination created havoc on Passage Island after he allowed Annie and Johanna to tie a rope around his waist and lower him down a rocky cliff to retrieve some bird eggs. Keeper Bowen and Larry's uncle, had to come to the rescue when the girls couldn't haul Larry back to the top—partly because he wouldn't let go of the eggs to grab onto the rocks and help pull himself up! This was one rescue that didn't make it into the keeper's log—and Larry's family didn't ever allow him to visit Passage Island again. Photograph courtesy of Anna Bowen Hoge

cow' that we got from the evaporated milk cans. To this day I can hear my mother say, 'Annie, go down to the basement and get the tin cow.' And to this day I do not like milk. My mother believed in hot cereal for breakfast, so we were forced to eat the stuff. She also believed in a 'spring tonic' made from molasses. We always got a spoonful of it in the spring—I guess it was supposed to keep us well. The only thing I can remember that I didn't like my father for was when he mixed the canned milk into our tonic!

"We didn't have chickens or cows; there weren't even any moose on our island. I guess when the last ice age was carving out and smoothing the rocks on Passage Island, the moose couldn't make the distance from Isle Royale, just four miles to our southwest. So we didn't have fresh meat of any kind except fish. Both Mother and Dad were great fishermen. Many hours were spent cleaning and smoking fish to be stored as our supply of meat."

Anna's family went to Copper Harbor for the three to four months during winter when ice blocked shipping on the Great Lakes and the light stations were shut down. While in Copper Harbor Anna attended regular school, but she encountered difficulty being accepted—she pronounced words differently, and she was ahead in some skills, and behind in some. All in all, Anna found it difficult emotionally and physically to be separated from her home on Passage Island. Her parents decided Anna should continue her education via correspondence using the educational workbooks issued by the U.S. government. "Traveling library" books that rotated among the light stations within the area also contributed to Anna's education. The portable solid-wood trifold bookcases contained the classics as well as *National Geographic* magazines. "I traveled the world on those rocks on Passage Island," Anna says about her childhood reading experiences.

"What I remember most about the island is the clean, cold water we drew from the lake for all our uses—even drinking," she continues. "And the rainbow colors of the lantern's prisms, and the beautiful colors of nature all around us in the flowers that grew right out of the rocks, and the cool ferns of the forest, and oh, yes! the painful stab of the devil's club plant hidden among the inviting moss and greenery of the forest's floor.

"I've often dreamed of the countless times Mother had us kids in the kitchen pulling taffy," Anna continues. "When the weather threatened or she was nervous about something, she never alarmed us. We just pulled that taffy until all was right with the world again."

Under President Franklin Delano Roosevelt in 1939, the U.S. Lighthouse Service merged with the U.S. Coast Guard. When Anna's father told her that they were being transferred full-time to the mainland to New Presque Isle Lighthouse, Anna was not happy. "How can I leave my island? Who will take care of the light for the passing ships and people? And who will take care of the fragile life here on the island?" she asked. Anna could not sleep until she figured out a way to leave part of herself behind to protect this home so dear to herself and her family. She decided to bury one of her most treasured possessions on the island.

When Keeper Vern Bowen and his family moved to New Presque Isle Lighthouse, Anna witnessed her father's transition from a man of importance in the U.S. Lighthouse Service to a maintenance man in the U.S. Coast Guard. New Presque Isle was the last lighthouse Vern Bowen served, and he died when Anna was only eighteen.

Anna Bowen grew up, married Ralph Hoge, and became a cancer-care nurse. Now retired and living in Kalamazoo, Michigan, Anna remains active in lighthouse activities. She is one of the founding members of the Great Lakes Lighthouse Keepers' Association and the Lake Superior Lighthouse Children's Association.

"It upsets me today that the curtains are no longer drawn to protect the fragile Fresnel lenses in the lighthouses," says Anna. "I think back to how my father and other keepers lived their lives around the work of the lights, but today that respect is gone. As soon as radio technology was developed for navigational aid, the lighthouses were automated—to me, this means 'abandoned.' How great it is that more and more people are learning the meaning behind these lighthouses and what a part of our history they are. Maybe somebody will go back to pulling those curtains. But when there isn't a live soul in the lighthouses, how can that happen?

"Dad hung the American flag first thing each morning. And it was a family affair to bring it down each evening." Anna speaks reverently about her father's lighthouse keeper uniforms. She especially liked the brass buttons and recently had them copied to give as mementos to people who know about and appreciate lighthouses.

Anna goes often to Old Presque Isle Lighthouse (just up the road from New Presque Isle Lighthouse where she once lived) to visit her longtime friend Lorraine Paris and to rest and re-energize from her ongoing battle with cancer. Why does this woman hold such esteem for a remote place so many years in her past? Anna talks about the strength she finds in water and beacons. She

Annie, a friend, sister Johanna, Billie, Sonny, and other passengers waiting for the boat to take them from Isle Royale to Passage Island, far out in Lake Superior

"A trip to the Michigan mainland came only a few times a year," Anna explains. "I loved to visit the city, but returning to my island was the happiest part of any trip." Photograph courtesy of Anna Bowen Hoge

scoops up a handful of lake water and touches her feverish shoulder while she talks of the rocks, the birds, and the energy in the surrounding beauty. She talks about the universal spirit, a continuum of energy—as the Great Lakes ebb and flow to reach the Atlantic, so the human spirit ebbs and flows to reach God.

Anna's father told her many times about the "little people" or "elves" who took care of Passage Island, and she believes in them. Like other lighthouse children, Anna appreciates nature, simplicity, loyalty, and pride in work. She knows that the human spirit is as real as the physical body and, like the body, needs nourishment that comes from one's life endeavors and appreciation of each of God's creations.

"Society puts up this blank wall and says, 'We are not interested,'" continues Anna. "So I didn't tell for a long time that I grew up in a lighthouse or on an island. But as I got older, I knew I had to share my past with my children and grandchildren—I would have to share with them my rich heritage and their future."

Anna talks about cancer, growing old, the child within her who visits Passage Island at will, and the fear of going back to visit Passage Island as an adult. "I wondered for forty-two years if I had just imagined this paradise. I was very nervous to return and open my eyes to exactly what did exist there. It represented my very being."

Grown-up Anna became ten-year-old Annie when she stepped off the boat onto Passage Island for the first time in more than four decades. She could hear her father singing and whistling and smell her mother's fresh cinnamon rolls. She could see her father dressed in his impressive U.S. Lighthouse Service uniform polishing the prisms of the beautiful lens, her mother fishing alone as welcome reprieve from the demanding duties as a lighthouse mother and wife, her baby brother testing the limits of his tethered line, her sister kicking her feet in the frigid waters of Lake Superior, and the whole family sitting together watching a Lake Superior sunset.

When Anna started digging up the treasure she had buried forty-two years earlier, she realized that she had given her prized possession as an offering to the island, much as the Indians had paid honor to the island through song, dance, and peace offerings. Legend says that long before the white man came, the Ojibwa ruled the nearby forests and paid homage to Nanibijou, the "Great Spirit," who lived on Mount McKay and watched to keep his people safe as they crossed the "Gitche Gumee" (Lake Superior). Nanibijou showed the Indians a prolific silver mine and told them that if any white man learned of this secret, they would die and he would turn to stone. A disloyal Indian did tell a white man, and as Nanibijou prophesied when the Indian and his companions were traveling across Lake Superior a violent storm broke out and they drowned. The next day a gigantic rock peninsula in the form of a Sleeping Giant rose up from the once-open waters of Thunder Bay–Nanibijou had indeed turned to stone. Anna often looked at the Sleeping Giant from her perch on Passage Island.

When Annie unearthed her buried treasure–an original Shirley Temple doll her grandmother had given her, a doll she loved as much as she loved herself–she put down the shovel. She decided to leave her precious offering where it was for her children, grandchildren, and those beyond. Removing it would be removing the essence of Passage Island and the heritage of the U.S. Lighthouse Service for her descendants. She also decided to make another trip to Passage Island, this time bringing her children and grandchildren with her "to add to the legacy and teach them to give back more treasure than they receive."

A few years after her first trip back to Passage Island, Anna's husband, children, and grandchildren accompanied her on her second journey back in time. They had the whole island to themselves for the day, and in keeping with her childhood tradition, the first thing they did was take a rope and run the American flag up a pole. Before they left the island, Anna's grandkids buried a treasure box near hers.

Anna felt great joy in sharing the peace, tranquility, and precious childhood memories of this remote island paradise with her family. She takes comfort in the fact that Passage Island "is too small and no longer needed for navigation" and so will most likely retain the pristine beauty of her childhood.

Memories of Passage Island continue strong in Anna. She returns again and again in her dreams to the rock where she lay as a child pondering the expanse of Lake Superior. In one frightening dream, she saw a "ship dying" on the rocks just below her favorite place. "I kept trying to warn it away from the rocks," she says. Later, while looking at the December 1996 issue of *Lake Superior Magazine*, she saw an article about a ship that had wrecked a few months earlier. She recognized the white vessel in the photographs as the one in her nightmares. Anna was sad and spoke reluctantly about that experience. "I feel as if there has been a death of a boat. Like my island, there's no one there to care."

Anna has felt a loss since the day she left Passage Island in 1943. She knows she will feel whole again once her spirit flies across the cold, blue Lake Superior waters to go home again, this time forever.

FAMILY RECIPE

Anna says, "I kept Mom's old recipe cards with fond memories. I can close my eyes at anytime and see her very clearly, and at Passage Island I thought I could smell the rolls when I returned after forty-two years. I loved them so when I was young Annie that I would once in a while eat a tiny piece of the yeast cake. Mom's recipe also stated 'a dab of this or a pinch of that.' She always set the bowl covered with a clean flour sack on the top shelf on the woodstove. Many times on her recipe she wrote, 'Time out for cup of coffee.' These fond memories are my greatest assets in life."

Anna's mom, Billie, served up a plateful of memories with her cinnamon rolls stacked high and steaming fresh from the stove on the kitchen windowsill of the Passage Island keeper's house. Anna now serves her mother's rolls to her grandchildren every Christmas. "I have had to change many things in Mom's recipe to be able to use it now—such as yeast cakes. The milk Mom used was canned milk—we called it the 'tin cow,' and she had to mix the evaporated milk with water. As for the baking temperature, Mom had a wood burner and knew how to test temperature. We never had fresh eggs on Passage Island, so I added an egg. Once in a while we had apples and nuts, and I use those often when I prepare these rolls."

MOM'S CINNAMON ROLLS

Rolls:
6$\frac{1}{4}$ to 6$\frac{3}{4}$ cups all-purpose flour
2 packages active dry yeast
2 cups milk
$\frac{1}{4}$ cup white sugar
$\frac{1}{4}$ cup butter or margarine
1$\frac{1}{2}$ teaspoons salt
1 egg

In a large bowl, combine 2$\frac{1}{2}$ cups flour and yeast; set mixture aside.
In a saucepan, heat and stir milk, sugar, butter, and salt until just warm. Add milk mixture to flour mixture.
Add egg and beat very well with wooden spoon; stir in as much of the remaining flour as you can.
Put dough on lightly floured surface and knead in enough flour to make a soft dough; shape dough into a ball. Put into lightly greased bowl, and lightly grease top of dough ball. Cover dough and let it rise in a warm place until it doubles in size.

Filling:
$\frac{1}{2}$ cup packed brown sugar
$\frac{1}{2}$ cup white sugar
$\frac{1}{4}$ cup all-purpose flour
1 tablespoon ground cinnamon
$\frac{1}{2}$ cup butter or margarine
2 cups finely chopped apples (optional)
1 cup chopped nuts (optional)

In a small bowl, combine brown sugar, white sugar, flour, and cinnamon. Cut in butter until mixture resembles coarse crumbs.

Punch the doubled dough ball down. Put dough on lightly floured surface, cover, and let rest for 10 minutes.

Grease a baking pan.

Roll dough into rectangle. Sprinkle with filling; add optional ingredients if desired. Roll from long side, jelly-roll style. Pinch to seal edges.

Cut dough crosswise into rolls, and place cut side down on greased pan. Cover and let rise in warm place until double in size.

Bake, uncovered, at 350° for approximately 40 minutes or until lightly browned and rolls sound hollow when lightly tapped.

Enjoy!

PASSAGE ISLAND LIGHT STATION is on Passage Island, part of Isle Royale National Park and the northernmost point of U.S. land in Lake Superior. During summer months, visitors can take an overnight boat trip to Isle Royale and from there another boat ride to Passage Island; reservations are a must. (Ice on Lake Superior prohibits trips to Passage Island during winter months.) The National Park Service operates an information center and bookstore at the landing dock on Isle Royale.

For information on transportation and accommodations contact Isle Royale National Park, 800 East Lakeshore Drive, Houghton, MI 49931; 906/482-0984.

ST. AUGUSTINE

CATS, PARACHUTES, AND SOUTHERN LIGHTHOUSES

Keeper Cardell D. Daniels came from the small fishing village of Wanchese on North Carolina's Outer Banks, as did nine of his contemporaries who served at neighboring southern light stations. He married Grace Tillett in Manteo, North Carolina, on April 27, 1917. The following year he took his bride to St. Augustine Light Station, where he began his U.S. Lighthouse Service career as the assistant keeper during World War I.

Throughout his thirty-two-year career, Keeper Daniels kept jockeying for better jobs and places for his family to live. Florida during the Great Depression turned out to be a good place for Cardell and Grace Daniels to raise their five children: Cardell D. "Cracker" Jr., Vera, Leroy, Leonard, and Wilma, who was born in her brothers' bedroom in the Ponce de Leon Inlet assistant keeper's house. That house has been named the Davis House in honor of Gladys Meyer Davis (see page 165). Wilma and Gladys are two of the few people still living who can make a lighthouse-birth claim.

Whenever the Daniels kids moved to a new light station, they lost no time getting down to the serious work of playing hard. Wilma and Cracker share some of their memories of "playing" at St. Augustine Lighthouse.

Cardell D. Daniels Sr. began his keeper's career in 1918 as a newlywed at St. Augustine Lighthouse. When World War I ended, he went to Norfolk to work in a shipyard and then rejoined the U.S. Lighthouse Service in 1927. One of the few keepers to have served more than a half dozen major lights on the East Coast, Cardell Daniels worked at Cape Hatteras, Jupiter Inlet, Ponce de Leon Inlet, St. Augustine, Hunting Island, Carys Fort Reef, Cape Canaveral, and Morris Island before his retirement at the new Charleston Lighthouse on Sullivans Island in 1947. Along with maintaining lighthouses, Cardell and his wife, Grace, raised five children, Cardell D. "Cracker" Jr. (born in 1920), Vera (1922), Leroy (1924), Leonard (1928), and Wilma (1931).

After a short tenure at Cape Hatteras Lighthouse, a position opened at Jupiter Inlet Light Station, and Keeper Daniels took advantage of the opportunity so Cracker and Vera could attend the nearby school and the family could go to church more easily. But not all went as smoothly as he hoped.

Jupiter Inlet Lighthouse had a long history of disaster. To begin with, it took four years to build the lighthouse because of the horrid seasonal heat and abundance of

Jupiter Inlet Lighthouse, Florida

pesky mosquitoes and other insects that generously shared germs. And within a year of its lighting in 1860, the Confederates put out the first-order lens. Then in the late 1920s, while the Daniels family lived in the keeper's house, a fire destroyed everything. The U.S. Lighthouse Service rebuilt the house, and Keeper Daniels, Grace, and the children moved into their brand-new home. Fate, however, had one more disaster in store for Jupiter Inlet. In 1926, almost like a grand finale, a hurricane twisted the keeper's house off its foundations, turning it completely around. "Yes," Cracker admits openly, "that was very scary.

"But I'll tell you about one of the most frightening things that's ever happened to me," he goes on excitedly. "You know, Jupiter is on a good-size hill. Well one day I was playing around with a car tire and decided to try riding inside it. The next thing I know, I'm rolling down the hill! And then I hit those LONG steps–BOOM! BOOM! BOOM! all the way down. I'm rolling so fast now, I can't stop. I rolled all the way onto the dock and down to the end, rolled off the dock, and SPLASH! into the water between two sailboats. I'm knocked so silly by now–I had to be hooked out like a drunk fish! My gosh, I'll never forget that!" Cracker laughs heartily, more than five decades after his wild tire ride.

After a couple of years of harrowing family adventures at Jupiter Inlet, Keeper Daniels won the appointment of principal keeper of Ponce de Leon Inlet Light Station, near Daytona Beach, Florida. Always concerned about their children's education, Cardell and Grace were pleased that a school bus came by the lighthouse to haul their young crew to the small school in Port Orange.

Ponce de Leon Inlet Lighthouse came with both a boathouse and a rowboat. Twelve-year-old Cracker quickly figured out that he could earn fifty cents to a dollar by rowing

(Back row) Vera and Cardell D. Jr. "Cracker," (front row) Cardell D. Sr., Grace, Wilma, Leonard (holding Smoky, the parachuting cat), and Leroy

Keeper Daniels kept jockeying for better positions and living conditions for his wife and children. In 1935 he landed the principal keeper's job at St. Augustine Light Station, a happy place to raise a family. Photograph courtesy of the Daniels family

tourists on fishing expeditions on the river by the lighthouse. Cracker, the consummate entrepreneur, also had a healthy clam business going. Again using the lighthouse rowboat, he would gather clams and earn a little extra if the market was right. Since the U.S. Lighthouse Service tabooed business ventures by lighthouse kids, Cracker and the other Daniels kids learned to be extremely discreet about guiding fishing trips and selling freshly dug clams.

An even greater entrepreneurial opportunity loomed on the horizon though, and the Daniels children lost no time in tending to business when the family moved to St. Augustine Light Station. Located on the mainland close to major tourist attractions, St. Augustine Lighthouse was a prime stopping place, and Wilma and Cracker soon got the tourist-guiding routine down to a fine science.

Even during the Great Depression northerners often escaped winter by coming

Keeper Cardell Daniels, Grace, and Wilma on a buoy that washed ashore during a rough storm in 1937

Principal Keeper Daniels tended St. Augustine Lighthouse as well as buoys and other navigational devices in the area. Storm winds and waves often wreaked havoc that demanded the keeper's immediate attention. Photograph courtesy of the Daniels family

to warm, sunny Florida, many of them stopping to tour magnificent St. Augustine Lighthouse. Naturally they would want to climb to the top of the tower, and seven-year-old Wilma and teenage Cracker would take turns acting as their personal guides. After the long climb up to the lantern room and a detailed rundown on the great Fresnel lens that came from Paris, the children led the tourists back down the steps to the lighthouse door where they kept a handy stash of postcards. Handing a tourist a "free" postcard never failed to produce a nickel or dime—or the biggest prize of all, a quarter. During Depression days, that was big money for a kid.

"It cost a dime for the movies in town, and a nickel would buy a drink, so we were able to see lots of movies," explained Wilma.

In addition to seeing movies, the two kids had other plans for the money they earned. Every aspect of the lighthouse fascinated Cracker, especially the height of the tower, and he spent most of his money on model airplanes. He always had something under construction in the lighthouse workroom.

Perhaps seeing Charlie Chaplin and his famous umbrella in a movie inspired Wilma to buy an umbrella—although using it as a parachute and jumping off the garage roof to see if it worked was probably Wilma's own idea. "It just turned inside out," says Wilma, who recalls landing in the soft sandy yard with her ruined umbrella in her hand.

Cracker had watched the whole thing out the workroom window, and his attention suddenly shifted from model airplanes to parachutes. Within a few days he had tested several model parachutes by dropping them from the lighthouse catwalk at the very top of the tower. He perfected a final prototype and was ready to try something big, when Wilma's cat, Smoky, just happened to casually stroll by the window.

Cracker's model parachute was just right for a cat, and so up to the top of the light-house they went. Cracker remembers standing on the appropriately named "catwalk" beside the magnificent first-order Fresnel lens and feeling some of the grandiosity that Einstein, Bell, and Ford must have felt just before demonstrating their great inventions. He carefully tied the unsuspecting cat to the parachute and let go. Fortunately for Cracker, the admiring audiences that came to see demonstrations by the other great inventors had not come to see his cat parachute—so not a soul other than himself saw Smoky drop from the top of the tower and float down the 160-plus feet to the ground.

All four of Smoky's feet were scrambling during his semi-free fall, and he hit the ground running, dragging Cracker's ingenious invention behind him. Once free of the parachute, Smoky tore off toward the distant dunes—and he didn't show up for dinner that evening.

Wilma went around the neighborhood calling, "Here Smoky, here kitty-kitty!" Her brother just looked at the ceiling when asked if he knew where Smoky had gone—of course he didn't know where the cat had gone. No one was asking why the cat went, they just were asking where the cat was. Although he didn't know exactly where

Five-year-old Wilma with a tourist at St. Augustine Light Station

Visitors always wanted to have their picture taken at historic St. Augustine Light Station, and the enterprising Daniels children were always ready to oblige when asked to pose with them. The flowers Grace Daniels lovingly planted added welcome touches of color and beauty to the front yard. Photograph courtesy of the Daniels family

Smoky was, Cracker surmised that the way the cat had taken off when he hit the ground, Smoky was a good way from the lighthouse by now.

About a month later Smoky came back. "Daddy said, 'Must have climbed in one of those tourist cars while you all were doing a tour. Smoky is a real smart cat to find his way back. Might have had to walk back from New Jersey, maybe even New York. He's a tough cat.' I couldn't have agreed more!" chuckles Cracker.

As he had learned early on, Cracker "discreetly" kept his cat parachute venture secret for more than fifty years. It was not until one night in 1993 at St. Augustine Lighthouse where Wilma and Cracker had been invited by Cullen Chambers, former director of the restored St. Augustine Light Station, that Cracker let the whole story slip out.

Wilma was astonished. "You didn't try it again," Wilma smugly stated.

Cracker wearing his mother's clothes at Halloween 1939

"This picture shows Cracker's happy-go-lucky personality," Wilma says. *"He dressed up in Mama's clothes for a Halloween skating party at the YMCA in St. Augustine in 1939."* Photograph courtesy of the Daniels family

"Oh, no, Pinky" said Cracker, using the name of endearment he always used for Wilma when they were kids. Gazing up at that same ceiling he had looked at some fifty or more years before, Cracker said, "I'd never do that again."

"You know, come to think of it, that cat disappeared for good awhile later," said Wilma. Cracker just looked at the ceiling, and Wilma thought she saw a faint smile on his face.

As war clouds gathered on the horizon in 1939, the U.S. Lighthouse Service merged with the U.S. Coast Guard as part of President Roosevelt's Reorganization Act. As a coast-guardsman Keeper Daniels became chief boatswain mate first class and later chief petty officer in charge of St. Augustine Light Station.

Leroy joined the navy and Leonard joined the army, but Cracker got turned down by the military—yet he was the first brother to see the enemy. While he was walking on the beach between the coast guard station and St. Augustine Lighthouse going home from work at dusk one night, he heard a tremendous explosion and saw a tanker burst into flames a few miles off the coast. As he watched the ship burn, he saw the dark shape of a conning tower break the surface of the ocean and a German submarine appear. For a terrible, anxious moment, Cracker was sure the enemy would take aim at the lighthouse, but apparently the U-boat crew just wanted to take a look at their prize and make sure the tanker had sunk, for the submarine quickly submerged. Fortunately for the Daniels family—and for future generations—the Germans did not destroy historic St. Augustine Lighthouse.

After World War II, though, neglect and vandals nearly succeeded in destroying what the Germans had not, and in 1969 the U.S. Coast Guard declared St. Augustine Light Station surplus property and put it up for sale. A suspicious fire gutted the keeper's house, and for the next ten years the site lay abandoned.

In 1980 the Junior Service League of St. Augustine took on the responsibility of restoring the light station and hired Cullen Chambers, restoration expert and historic preservation specialist, to organize and supervise the project. State funding plus a major fundraising drive provided the money to restore the site to its former glory, with more than a third of a million dollars spent on the first-order Fresnel lens. The restoration, completed in April 1994, has proved to be one of the most successful ever undertaken.

Both Cracker and Wilma still live near St. Augustine Light Station. The keeper's house that they once called home now houses a museum as well as a bookstore/gift shop. The Daniels children no longer serve as personal tour guides, but visitors are welcome to climb the restored 1874 lighthouse tower.

FAMILY RECIPE

Wilma Daniels Thompson still remembers the wonderful meals her mother prepared in the keeper's kitchen. Her mother's favorite creation was chicken and dumplings. Wilma says, "The chickens were best because my mom raised them herself, and she always had fresh eggs too. I still have Mama's rolling pin and use it for good luck when I make this recipe!"

MAMA'S CHICKEN AND DUMPLINGS

1 whole chicken	Scant cup water
3 cups flour	1 teaspoon salt
2 eggs	Pepper to taste

In a big pot boil the chicken until done. Take the chicken out of the pot and debone it; make sure there are no bones left in the broth. Put the chicken aside; allow broth to simmer.

Mix flour, eggs, water, salt, and pepper. Flour board and roll out dough using a floured rolling pin on a surface covered with waxed paper with some flour sprinkled on it. Cut dough into long narrow strips.

Bring broth to boiling. Drop dough strips into boiling broth and cook until plump. Add chicken to broth and dumplings, and let stew together for a while.

Keeper Cardell and Grace Daniels pose for a formal picture in St. Augustine, Florida, in 1941.

During his almost thirty-two-year career that included numerous light stations and spanned World Wars I and II, Cardell Daniels served as keeper of St. Augustine Lighthouse in 1918 and again from 1935 to 1945. He transferred into the U.S. Coast Guard in 1941, earning first the rank of chief boatswain mate first class and later chief petty officer in charge of the light station. Photograph courtesy of the Daniels family

ST. AUGUSTINE LIGHT STATION is near downtown St. Augustine, Florida. To reach the light station, take the bridge toward St. Augustine Beach. The lighthouse, with its white and black spiral stripes and red lantern roof, is visible from the bridge on the left side of the highway.

The Junior League of St. Augustine has beautifully restored both the lighthouse and the classic keeper's house, which now houses an excellent museum and one of the best lighthouse shops in America. Visitors may climb the lighthouse tower.

For more information contact the Junior League of St. Augustine, 81 Lighthouse Avenue, St. Augustine, FL 32084; 904/829-0745.

Photograph by Bob and Sandra Shanklin

CAPE FLATTERY
CHRISTMAS MEMORIES

Ed Heikla and his wife, Ina, struggled as a post–World War I couple with two baby girls. In 1927 Keeper Heikla courageously accepted an assignment at Cape Flattery on Tatoosh Island, the northwesternmost point of the continental United States. Cape Flattery had earned a reputation of being one of the most lonely lighthouse posts, a notoriety heightened by the recent suicide of a young coastguardsman who could no longer take the isolation.

When the lighthouse tender delivered the Heiklas and their baggage, chickens, and cow to the remote island, Ina felt apprehensive about being so far away from any other settlement and especially from medical care for her young daughters. But like other lighthouse families, the Heiklas learned to be self-sufficient, and being isolated made their family bonds all the stronger. Living at Cape Flattery became a never-to-be-forgotten experience for Keeper Heikla, Ina, Doris, and Marian.

Almost seventy years later Marian can still see, hear, feel, and taste the details that punctuated her days on Tatoosh Island. She remembers living "under the lighthouse tower" in a duplex-style dwelling and sharing a staircase with another family to reach the upstairs bedrooms. She remembers the island families joining together to celebrate special occasions. She remembers their cow falling off the edge of the island onto the rocks and into the sea and the men trying to pull the cow back up with ropes and boats—and the cow being too badly hurt and having to be destroyed. She remembers "Uncle Jim" rowing his little boat from the Makah Indian village on the "faraway" coast of Washington and bringing mail and fresh foods. Most of all Marian remembers the Christmas her family spent at Cape Flattery, the Christmas she was five years old.

I t was magical," Marian sighs with longing, still vividly recalling Christmas Eve 1928. "My sister, Doris, and I had a hard time going to sleep the night before," she continues. "The sweep of the lighthouse beacon, the scream of the wind, the warning moan of the foghorn, and the creaking of the stairs kept us awake. We got out of bed and tiptoed downstairs to the decorated tree. We touched it and made a wish for good weather so Uncle Jim, our Makah Indian friend, could bring our Christmas packages and supplies in

(Back row, from left) Grandmother Kisa Edvard, Marian Heikla, Cousin Kathryn Damito, and Grandfather Johan Edvard; (front row, from left) Cousin Audrey Damito and Doris Heikla
Marian spent much of her childhood with these and other members of her close-knit Finnish family. She developed a strong sense of her Old-World heritage and still enjoys sharing her family's traditional customs with her children, grandchildren, and friends. Photograph courtesy of Marian Heikla Smith

his boat and so Santa Claus could bring the dolls Doris and I asked for.

"I remember waking up Christmas Eve morning and hearing the wind whip and whistle outside my second-story bedroom," says Marian. "The sounds of the wind and foghorn used to frighten me, but I had gotten used to them. I started snuggling back down under the warm quilts next to Doris, who was still asleep, when I suddenly remembered what day it was. I sat straight up in bed in a panic–if it was too windy and foggy, Uncle Jim wouldn't be able to land his boat–Christmas would be ruined!"

Five-year-old Marian tiptoed to the window. One glimpse confirmed her worst fears–the sky looked gray and unfriendly, thick fog hid the outline of the Washington mainland, and the lighthouse flag strained at its mast with each gust of wind. She slipped out of her cozy nightgown and into the layers of warm clothing her mother had laid out the night before and got downstairs to the warm kitchen as fast as she could.

Her mother, Ina, was already preparing the food for the traditional Finnish holiday celebration, which lasted from Christmas Eve until midnight December 26th, the feast day of St. Stephen. During the next two days Ina would serve her family and friends Old-World foods–baked cod with allspice-flavored cream sauce, boiled vegetables from last summer's garden, and rye bread as well as black bread, *kovaa leipää* (hardtack), *nisua* (coffee cake), and *kropsua pannukakku* (toasted coffee cake). If they were lucky, Uncle Jim would bring them a fresh ham along with their Christmas packages. But Marian's favorite part of the Christmas Eve meal was dessert–animal-shaped spiced cookies and, the final treat, oranges, apples, and dates that had been hung on the trimmed fir tree, ready to be "picked."

Marian remembers that her father was also in the kitchen that Christmas Eve morning. Dressed in his dark-blue keeper's uniform with the brass buttons decorated with lighthouses, Keeper Ed Heikla was the most handsome man in the world in Marian's admiring eyes. "Do you think Uncle Jim can land the boat today?" Marian blurted out. The words had escaped before she could stop them. Now she had done it–the worry would become reality, she just knew it–and it would be all her fault!

New Dungeness Light Station
Superintendent Isaac Smith simultaneously supervised the construction of Cape Flattery Light Station, at the western end of the Strait of Juan de Fuca, and New Dungeness Light Station, at the eastern end. At both light stations, the lighthouse tower rises through the roof of the main house. Marian says that flotsam and jetsam, like that shown in this picture, often washed ashore when the Heikla family lived on Tatoosh Island. Photograph courtesy of U.S. Coast Guard Archives

Marian, on the rocks and obviously not happy about it

Despite this picture, Marian remembers that most of the time she enjoyed playing along the cliffs of Tatoosh Island. "My mother was very daring," Marian says. "She would walk us kids along the edge of the island and allow us to sit, dangling our legs over the cliffs." Photograph courtesy of Marian Heikla Smith

CAPE FLATTERY

Cape Flattery Light Station, Tatoosh Island, Washington, 1928
The outcroppings of rock at the mouth of the Strait of Juan de Fuca spell sure disaster for unwary ships, making the need for a lighthouse obvious. Cape Flattery Light Station, completed in 1858 and one of the first of sixteen lights built along the West Coast, marks the entrance to the deceptively dangerous strait between Washington and Vancouver Island that leads to Puget Sound and Seattle. For many years a weather station and a U.S. Coast Guard radio station also occupied Tatoosh Island, which marks the northwesternmost tip of the continental United States. Photograph courtesy of U.S. Coast Guard Archives

Cape Flattery Light Station prior to the turn of the twentieth century
The Makah Indians resented the U.S. government building a light station at one of their favorite summer fishing spots, and the construction crew erected an armed fortification in case of attack. Over the years, however, the Makah Indians became good friends with the lighthouse station families. Known for their outstanding boat-handling skills, "Uncle Jim" and other Makahs rowed small boats to the island, bringing supplies and serving as occasional transportation back to the mainland. Photograph courtesy of The National Archives

"Now don't worry, Little One," her father replied. "Things will go as they should, and it isn't for you or me to try to control them. God will provide, and we will be thankful for what He gives us." Her mother had added, "Christmas will happen, Marian, because our family is together, and we will make the best of it, no matter what today brings."

Doris had come downstairs in time to hear Marian asking about Uncle Jim. *"Hauskaa Joulua!"* she called from the doorway, trying to cheer up everybody, especially Marian. Doris loved her little sister and helped her parents take care of her. Since Marian was one of the youngest children on the island, she did not get to participate in the daily activities such as school. This year Doris had introduced Marian to the teacher, Mrs. Willis, who had invited her to sit in the classroom and do as much as she was able. She had even given Marian a small part in the Christmas play.

"It was really exciting to perform for such a large audience–five families!" Marian says. Her father had even told her, "Break a leg!" for good luck just as she was opening the door to go to the schoolhouse for the play. When she turned to smile at her father, a gust of wind slammed the massive lighthouse door on her little finger. Marian remembers screaming from both the pain and the fear of not being able to play her part. "Mother chipped ice from the water bucket outside the door and Doris got bandages," Marian says, "and Father held me close to him to shut out the hurt." After her finger was bandaged, Marian stood up, straightened her costume, and went on to make her island debut.

All had ended well the day of the play, but Marian wasn't so sure about Christmas Eve. "The weather is bad today," she moaned. A few minutes later Father said it was time to go out and watch for Uncle Jim. Doris and Marian sprinted upstairs to get their coats and boots. "Maybe, just maybe, everything will be all right," Marian whispered to herself.

Marian and her older sister Doris

Marian and Doris enjoyed playing on this sidewalk, one of the few smooth surfaces at Cape Flattery Light Station. Photograph courtesy of Marian Heikla Smith

The girls dragged their parents as fast as they could to join the other island families gathered at the tram that led down to the Cape Flattery landing. Betty and Lois Myers held hands in anticipation, while Bobby and Ralph Wilhelm played a rough game of tag. Enid Boothe and Betty Koegler stood stoically together, not wanting to take part in such childish behavior. Stephen Cowan and Lawrence Myers took great pleasure in annoying Enid and Betty in between shadowboxing around their parents.

Marian remembers being concerned about the strong wind and the tall waves that Christmas Eve. "There seemed to be a constant clash of wills between the elements at this rocky point," she says. "There always seemed to be rough seas, stormy weather, and dense fog. The foghorn moaned for hours, even days at a time, just as it moaned that Christmas Eve," she continues. "Tatoosh Island seemed so far away from everything that foggy day. Life on the island could be very lonely at times, but that isolation also made me feel very special in my family's own world."

She remembers hearing someone shout, "Here he comes!" She and Doris squinted and strained to see the small craft dodging the high waves as it made its way toward them. Everyone fell silent and used body language to help Uncle Jim reach the island. Between the clouds of fog, they watched him struggle with the small craft laden with packages. They saw him steer leeward to avoid the stronger winds and crests—and then they saw him turn away from the island. Someone voiced what all of them had been fearing, "He's headed back to the mainland."

Marian can still feel her heart sinking as the entire entourage turned and headed back toward the lighthouse. Quietly one person began singing "Joy to the World," and slowly others joined in. "Despite our disappointment," Marian remembers, "Doris and I started singing too. And as we got close to our house, we saw something that our sad eyes could not believe. Coming down the lighthouse steps was a man dressed in red and carrying a bag slung over his shoulder. It couldn't be, but it was—Santa Claus!"

Santa handed each of the boys a hand-carved wooden wagon and a horse with movable parts, and he gave each of the girls a doll, not the ones they had hoped for but every bit as valuable as if Tiffany had made them. "The gifts Santa gave us that foggy Christmas Eve seemed more wonderful than all the toys in all the stores and catalogs in the world," says Marian. "Even though we noticed, we didn't say anything about the dolls being made from the same cloth as some of our clothes and the curtains we pulled to protect the lens of the lighthouse. And everyone was delighted when Santa reached into

his sack and pulled out oranges, apples, and figs—fresh fruit was a real treat," recalls Marian. "Clutching our treasures we thanked Santa and then ran home to get warm."

Back in their kitchen, the Heiklas gathered around the fir tree trimmed

Doris and Marian in front of the cistern that held rainwater

Ina Heikla, who was known for her handiwork, made dolls for her girls and other children for Christmas. "Mom also made the hats and coats we have on in this picture," Marian comments. Photograph courtesy of Marian Heikla Smith

Cape Flattery Light Station, two days before Christmas 1897
Cape Flattery looked much like this in 1928 when the Heiklas lived in the keeper's house. Marian still remembers that wind-whipped Christmas Eve and the utter disappointment of watching "Uncle Jim" struggle in vain to reach Tatoosh Island in his small boat filled with gifts. She also remembers the best Christmas present of all that year—the magical appearance of an unexpected but most-welcome visitor. Photograph courtesy of The National Archives

with Finnish decorations handed down from generation to generation. "The apples and other fresh fruit, candies, paper flags, and cotton and tinsel decorations came to life as my father carefully lit the candles secured to the branches," remembers Marian. "I loved looking at that Christmas tree."

Had the family lived in Finland instead of on Tatoosh Island, they would all have gone to the sauna and then put on clean clothes for Christmas Eve dinner. And on Christmas Day they would have attended the traditional church service, raced their neighbors afterward in their horse-drawn wagon to see who had the fastest horse in the community, and spent the rest of the holiday visiting friends and family members. "But on this lonely island where we were the only Finns," Marian says, "my parents just wished happiness and peace for us and our neighbors.

"There was a knock on the kitchen door, and we all went quickly to see what other surprises were coming. Outside were four boys with darkened faces and dressed in white robes and holding a star-shaped lantern. They were the *Tahti Pojat,* or Star Singers," explains Marian. "They caroled and made the gestures of writing symbols on the sides of the houses they visited as a sign that the families were blessed and no harm would come to them. What a thrill it was for us that the other families on the island would honor us by acting out this Scandinavian Yuletide custom."

A little while later Marian whispered to Doris, "I know what we can do to make this the best Christmas ever." She led Doris upstairs, and the two girls scrambled to finish a special project before Christmas Eve dinner.

After dinner Marian and Doris helped their parents clear the living room floor for the upcoming music. "We fell asleep that night listening to the adults downstairs. They were dancing, talking, and eating Mother's wonderful cake," says Marian.

Loud shouting and hurried footsteps woke the two girls Christmas morning, and by the time they were dressed and out the door, Uncle Jim had made a safe landing with the packages everyone had longed for yesterday but had now all but forgotten. "Don't let Uncle Jim leave before we get down there!" Marian and Doris yelled, struggling to run as fast as they could without dropping the box they were carrying between them.

Keeper Heikla helped Uncle Jim climb out of the small boat he had amazingly landed in yet another day's rough seas and asked him to wait for Marian and Doris to come. "Here, Uncle Jim," Marian and Doris told Uncle Jim as they handed him the box. "This is for your girls. Doris and I made all of it ourselves. *Hauskaa Joulua!* That's 'Merry Yule!' in Finnish."

Later their father had asked the girls what was in the box. "I told him that Mother had given us permission to share one of the dolls Santa brought us, and that we had used the Sears catalog to make paper dolls and clothes for his little girls," Marian said. "And after a LOT of thinking, we came up with the best gift we could send them—an apple and an orange from our tree, one of our spiced cookie horses, and a tinsel star."

Before the next Christmas, the Heiklas moved to Grays Harbor Lighthouse in Westport, about halfway down the coast of Washington. "I remember how seasick my mother and Doris were on the lighthouse tender when we moved to Grays Harbor, but my dad and I ate strawberry shortcake with the crew and really enjoyed the fresh berries," says Marian. "The ship came as close as it could to the beach, and then the coastguardsmen at Westport carried us through the surf to shore."

Marian liked Westport. "It was an actual little town with cement streets, houses, stores, and many new children to play with. We really enjoyed the grass—even the rough beach grass—so off went the shoes. And I would cry when I had to put them back on! Grays Harbor Lighthouse stood alone among the sand dunes. It was and still is very beautiful. I used to go up the circular stairs in the evening and pull open the blinds while my father started that gorgeous third-order light revolving."

In 1930 Marian's father decided to leave his career with the U.S. Lighthouse Service and work with her grandfather in the cranberry industry, which he had pioneered in

Mr. and Mrs. Art Wilhelm and the Heiklas at a picnic on the beach
"Families living on the island would get together for picnics and dances and playing cards,"
Marian remembers. Photograph courtesy of Marian Heikla Smith

Grayland, Washington. "But I never did get far from government service or the ocean," says Marian. "During World War II I joined the Women Marines and did teletype and code work. After the war, there was college and then marriage and three children. We moved from the beach at Washington State to southern Oregon and have raised our children here beside the ocean.

"I love lighthouses. My heart cries when I hear of the shabby conditions and the bad happenings to these beautiful public treasures," Marian concludes. She and her husband, Don Smith, live in Brookings, Oregon. Both of them are members of the Oregon Chapter of the U.S. Lighthouse Society and actively support lighthouse restoration projects.

FAMILY RECIPES

Marian is raising her grandchildren, like her children, in the traditional Finnish customs. She enjoys making this Old-World breakfast treat, which she remembers her mother making for her and Doris in the keeper's kitchen at Cape Flattery on Christmas Eve 1928.

KROPSUA PANNUKAKKU

1 cup flour   3/4 cup milk
3/4 teaspoon salt   3 eggs

Combine flour, salt, and milk, and stir until smooth. Beat the eggs slightly, and add to flour mixture. Pour into a greased cast-iron or long cake pan. Preheat oven to 450°; put pan in over, and lower temperature to 350°. Bake about 15 minutes.

Cut into squares. Serve with butter and syrup or sprinkle sugar on top.

SUGAR COOKIES

1/2 cup shortening   1/2 teaspoon salt
1 cup sugar   1/4 cup milk
1 egg   1/2 teaspoon lemon juice
2 cups sifted flour   or vanilla
1 teaspoon baking powder

Cream together shortening and sugar. Add egg, and beat until smooth.

Combine flour, baking powder, and salt. Combine milk and lemon or vanilla, and add to shortening mixture alternately with flour mixture. Roll out dough on floured board and cut into circles. Bake at 400° for 7 to 10 minutes.

APPLE CAKE WITH SAUCE

Cake:

4 cups diced apples	2 cups flour
2 cups sugar	2 teaspoons baking soda
2 beaten eggs	1 teaspoon salt
½ cup oil	2 teaspoons cinnamon
2 teaspoons vanilla	

Combine diced apples and sugar.
Combine eggs, oil, and vanilla. Sift together flour, baking soda, salt, and cinnamon; add to egg mixture, and mix well. Stir in apples and sugar. Bake at 350° for 50 to 60 minutes.

Sauce:
⅓ cup butter
¾ cup whipping cream
1 cup brown sugar

Combine ingredients in saucepan, and bring to boil. Remove from heat, and let cool for 10 minutes. Serve sauce over cut cake. Reheat leftover sauce as needed.

CAPE FLATTERY LIGHT STATION stands on Tatoosh Island, which marks the northwestern corner of the forty-eight contiguous United States as well as the entrance to the Strait of Juan de Fuca. The dangerous, spiraling currents in the strait have sent many ships crashing into the rocks of this narrow waterway. Unfortunately Cape Flattery Lighthouse is closed to the public.

GRAYS HARBOR LIGHTHOUSE, the tallest lighthouse on the Washington Coast, was built in 1898 and stands in a field of wildflowers on the sand dunes in Westport. Signs on U.S. 101 mark the route to Westport Coast Guard Station and the lighthouse. A small overlook on Ocean Avenue in Westport offers a good view of the octagonal tower. For more information contact the Westport Maritime Museum, 2201 Westhaven Drive, P.O. Box 1074, Westport, WA 98595; 360/268-0078.

Old Mackinac Point Light Station,
Michigan

HURON ISLAND
OLD MACKINAC POINT
LIGHTS OF THE GREAT LAKES

When jobs were scarce in 1932, John Peter Campbell, a twice-decorated Purple Heart Veteran of World War I, accepted his first U.S. Lighthouse Service assignment. In 1939, with the winds of another world war blowing strong across the Atlantic from Europe, Keeper Campbell and all the other "older" keepers faced losing their jobs when the U.S. Coast Guard absorbed the lighthouse service as part of military preparations. The coast guard, which was composed of mostly young men, allowed younger keepers to retain their jobs with either civilian status or an equivalent military title but retired most of the veteran keepers. Keeper Campbell fortunately kept his job and served a total of more than thirty years, including posts as first assistant keeper at Grassy Island in the Detroit River close to where it flows into Lake Erie, boatswain mate first class at Huron Island in Lake Superior, keeper at Old Mackinac Point in the Straits of Mackinac, and finally keeper at Point Betsie in Frankfort, Michigan.

Keeper Campbell and his wife, Edna, raised six children, five daughters and son Richard, better known as Dick. "My heart has always been near the lighthouses where I worked with my dad," says Dick, who generously shares his childhood memories.

In late December 1941 eleven-year-old Dick Campbell anxiously scanned the main road in L'Anse, Michigan, watching for signs of a car or bus that might be bringing his dad home for Christmas. "The U.S. Lighthouse Service tried to get the keepers off the last thing before the holiday. Sometimes it was the day before Christmas, and sometimes it was Christmas Day. The tender would take them up to Houghton. This was before we had a radio, so we didn't know when they were coming. Many a Christmas was spent just watching for Dad to come home."

Like his mother and sisters, Dick kept hoping that the lighthouse tender had been able to reach Huron Island and pick up Assistant Keeper John Campbell and bring him to the mainland before ice on Lake Superior blocked the way. The weather had been colder and the storms heavier than normal the past two months, and the lake had already started to freeze.

"There was no school on Huron Island," says Dick. Keeper Campbell tried to get ashore once a week, but bad weather often prevented it. "So Christmas was special for the family, together for the first time since the beginning of the school year," adds Dick.

The family really looked forward to summertime when they could all be together on Huron Island. Dick got to spend part of one school year with his dad on the island too—but not entirely by choice. He broke his left arm one November, and since he is left-handed, his teacher encouraged his mother to let him do his schoolwork at home. Used to being active, Dick found being home all day extremely boring, so his father suggested he come out to Huron Island until his arm healed.

Dick agreed to go even though he had several reasons for concern. Since all the women and children had left the island for the school year, not only would he be the only "child," but also men would be doing all the cooking. The closest town was 14 miles away from the island. And he would experience firsthand the gales of November. "Few people who live on land realize the kinds of storms that happen on the lake. When I was a young boy on Huron Island, I had never seen ferocious weather such as the wild lake. The big waves

Keeper John Peter Campbell

Dick's father, Keeper John P. Campbell, served at Grassy Island (at the mouth of the Detroit River where it flows into Lake Erie), Huron Island (in Lake Superior), and Point Betsie (on the Michigan coast of Lake Michigan). He also served as the last keeper at Old Mackinac Point, which closed in 1958 when radar technology and the completed Mackinac Bridge (if mariners couldn't see the bridge, it was assumed they should not be plying the straits) eliminated the need for the lighthouse. Keeper Campbell had kept the light station in mint condition, and the lack of care shown by the government workers who dismantled it appalled both him and his son Dick. Fortunately for future generations they were able to rescue many of the unique items that were so much a part of daily life in the historic lighthouse. Photograph courtesy of the Campbell family

Huron Island Light Station, Michigan

were unbelievable. The spray from the breakers reached above the 150-foot cliff on one side of the island.

"The weather in the spring and fall got crazy—wind, rain, snow, and fog," continues Dick. "The foghorn would go twenty-four to thirty hours straight. We'd get to where we carried on a conversation in between the blast of the foghorn! People on land wondered why we would automatically pause between phrases when we talked. They just needed to spend a few days on the island with the foghorn to shape their speech patterns."

That November Dick served as Huron Island's unofficial assistant keeper. Like his dad, Keeper James Collins, and Second Assistant Martin Peterson, he drank canned Carnation condensed milk and ate boiled potatoes, smoked ham, oatmeal, and "lots of fish," he recalls. "The men tried to make bread and biscuits," Dick tells with some mischief. "I remember one time when it was my father's turn to cook. As you know, biscuits sometimes do not rise properly in cool weather, and these turned out rather flat. About halfway through the meal, Martin, who was hard of hearing, asked for some more 'cookies' and helped himself to the biscuits. Several times he said to my father,

'Your cookies are really good.'

"After a full season at the light station, there was always tension among the men and few words were spoken at mealtime. Finally after several remarks about the 'cookies' and several reminders from my father that they were 'biscuits'—all of which Martin didn't hear, my father exploded. I thought they would come to blows. At the time, I didn't find it very funny and thought it a serious situation. In later years it became a family joke and very amusing—especially when biscuits were served. Even today, when my wife's biscuits don't rise, they become 'John's cookies.' "

Dick remembers that his father also made up large batches of pancakes and stored them in the Mother's Oats box in a cool place in the keeper's kitchen. Those pancakes were often used for making sandwiches since a trip to the "local" grocery meant several hours and a boat ride of several miles.

Keeper John Campbell's wife, Edna, wearing her husband's U.S. Lighthouse Service coat and cap

Dick Campbell remembers his mother being a real trouper. Since the island light stations his dad served didn't have schools, Dick and his sisters lived with their mother on the mainland during the school year. "It was a special time of year for the family to be together during the summer," says Dick. His mother was glad to be reunited with his dad, but she was not always thrilled about living on an island with six children. "Years later when my mother told about living at a lighthouse, I often wondered what she really thought about it." Photograph courtesy of the Campbell family

As Dick looks at old family pictures and shares more memories of growing up as a keeper's son, he mentions over and over again that the lighthouse keepers never forgot the importance of their jobs. Many bones of men and ships lie at the bottom of the Great Lakes due to early winter storms, completely unpredictable and often vicious, that Dick remembers from his childhood. Most ship owners took their ships off the Great Lakes before the icy northern winds swooped over the still-warm lake waters and produced the "gales of November." Gordon Lightfoot immortalized those late-fall storms in his song about the great *Edmund Fitzgerald*, the pride of the lakes in 1975 that succumbed to 20- and 30-foot-tall watery hills and deep troughs in a sudden and deadly storm.

Dick emphasizes that while the Great Lakes lighthouses were always of supreme importance to America's shipping industry, they were crucial during the war years for the safe passage of ships, big and small, loaded with precious iron ore and copper at the "lakehead" at Duluth and Two Harbors, Minnesota, on their way to the steel mills at Detroit, Cleveland, Gary, and Buffalo. Their course steered them south and eastward through the canal at Houghton to Jacobsville, Michigan. Continuing east, they came close to the Huron Mountain Range. Keeper James Collins, First Assistant Keeper John Campbell, and Second Assistant Keeper Martin Peterson made sure Huron Island Lighthouse shone bright no matter what the weather to warn ships away from their rocky post about 6 miles off the coast of Michigan's Upper Peninsula.

The keepers also made sure the lighthouse shone bright for the coast guard inspectors. "Cleanliness and everything being in its place were the most important things the inspector checked for–I learned that as a little kid. Another thing was that the inspectors didn't like children around so we had to get lost when an inspection was going on. We could be wringing wet and in need of dry clothes when he came along, but we just got out of sight!" Dick tells with a big laugh and a glint in his blue eyes.

"You would hear through the grapevine that the inspector was possibly due during a certain week. So we kids were expected to help watch. And watch. The inspector flew a special flag, so we could identify him coming at least in time to get final details taken care of. You couldn't possibly take care of all that was needed in just a few minutes. No, that took lots of constant work. But knowing about when sure helped. Every detail was laid out concerning an inspection. Machinery work orders, foghorn display, even where the daily keeper's log was to be placed," Dick recalls.

"There were lots of politics involved with keepers," he continues. "It seemed each was known throughout the islands. When a keeper came to a light, a lot was known about whether he was a 'good' guy or a 'bad' guy. When an inspector came it could be touchy if the inspector didn't like a particular keeper. There were five or six different inspectors. One might particularly inspect machinery, another buildings. They'd walk around the grounds with a clipboard and note anything wrong. Afterward a final report was written, and some of it was foolish. If we knew the inspector was prejudiced in some way for or against one of our keepers, we didn't even expect to get a good report. It was just like being in the military, you knew they'd find something wrong. Just like when I was in the military, I would tell my wife, 'I know I'm doing something wrong, but I don't know what!' " he says, laughing.

"Once my sister left her shoes on the stairs, and the keepers were called down for that. There were six of us kids, and anything might have happened. The inspector even checked under the beds—we could get 'wrote up' for even that. I remember once an inspector saw a streak or two on the ceiling where we had washed it. He suggested washing in the other direction the next time," Dick says, shaking his head at the ludicrous remark made many decades ago.

"Everything had to be painted—every year," he continues. "Whether it needed it or not, it had to be painted. And everything had its color. If you went from one lighthouse to another, they all looked the same. In the keeper's house, for instance, upstairs had a color and downstairs had another. The lighthouse service varied colors over the years. Of course when the coast guard took over, everything was painted green. So when spring arrived, here came all this paint—gallons and gallons of paint."

Dick remembers that his mother was not thrilled about the lack of "modern" conveniences on Huron Island. "We had no running water," he explains. "We had an outside privy. A brick one. We have pictures of it! It was brick, just like the house, with a metal roof. I remember it was a three-holer, with a small hole on the side for children and naturally, the Sears Roebuck catalog for one of the only conveniences we enjoyed! This one sat on the edge of a high rock cliff with a three-plank walk to it. A large wooden plank box was made each year and inserted in the lower back. Once a year the box was pushed overboard into the lake." Pretty efficient spring cleaning.

"We had no refrigeration at the beginning, and then later we had it," Dick adds. "At first we didn't have anything to be kept cold—food was dried or packaged to make it last a long time. There were a lot of wild rabbits on the island but we didn't eat them. Some lighthouses had chickens and other animals, but we didn't. A goat might have survived there, but nothing else could! There wasn't even enough dirt for a garden. We had quite a few berries like thimble berries that are quite rare on the Upper Peninsula and delicious. When picked they look like a large red thimble. There were a few huckleberries too, but little else grew on the island. It certainly wasn't a place for a farmer."

Dick mentions that a lighthouse keeper had to be a jack-of-all-trades. He had to know how to keep the light burning, fog equipment running, the boat repaired, and on and on. "Once a year a tender was sent 'round to handle the jobs that required special tools and equipment. But other than that, a keeper had to do all in his power to keep everything running its best," Dick says.

"The regulations on paperwork were piles thick—the government had a regulation for every move a keeper made," Dick explains. "Take paintbrushes, for instance. Each station was 'classed' according to its size and amount of equipment. The size and importance of your station determined if you got say, ten or twenty paintbrushes. Everything had to be inventoried. And this is one thing that always got me—when something wore out, you didn't throw it away. I guess the government didn't trust anyone. So when the inspector came, he inventoried shovels or whatever equipment the keeper was asking to be replaced. When a paintbrush was unusable ... and that is what they were, unusable, they were turned in and traded for a new one after inventory, after inspector approval.

"In fact, instead of throwing away a brush after several uses, the keepers used to fill a big copper ket-

Three-year-old Dick Campbell with thirteen-year-old Jane (left) and six-year-old Helen at Grassy Island Light Station in 1933
"This was such a happy time for our family, especially my mother, because we were together as a family," says Dick, "even though my mother was not impressed when she first saw this lighthouse—there were all of us kids and a small lighthouse and no modern conveniences." Photograph courtesy of the Campbell family

tle with lye and boil the brushes to clean them," says Dick, racing on with details about the workaday routine. "They boiled the brushes in lye because the kerosene couldn't be used, it was so valuable. In fact, the oil for the lamp was something like kerosene, but I remember as a youngster hearing it called 'ltb'—that's 'long time burning.' It was refined better so it wouldn't give off as much smoke as pure kerosene. It was the cleanest burning fuel I've ever seen.

"The oil for burning in the lamp didn't have as much carbon in it. And allotment for

Three-year-old Diana Dawn and five-year-old Kathleen at Huron Island Light Station in 1939
"Huron Island is only about a mile long and a quarter mile wide, and when your home is basically a pile of rocks, there aren't many activities to get involved in—we engaged in what you call 'creative play,' " says Dick. "There was no shallow water, and we all learned to swim there—and I don't remember ever seeing a life jacket. Lake Superior is cold, but we dove in regularly anyway." Photograph courtesy of the Campbell family

the station was based on previous years' inventory. The keeper was expected to keep to that allotment–or even better–under the amount allowed in the past for supplies like paint, oil, and coal. Even if there were extreme conditions, you had to make do."

He continues, "One railroad car of coal was equal to sixty tons. At Huron Island, the lighthouse tender would bring the coal packed in sacks. At Old Mackinac Point, where Dad was keeper from 1951 to 1958, a truck brought our supply and put most of it in the basement of the house. The rest was piled in the yard, and we kids had to move it to a storage area. And no, we didn't get paid for that. Can you imagine moving the better part of a train car of coal?! That's the kind of work we kids were expected to do.

"But I wanted to help," Dick adds. "When you're raised in it, it's just part of your life.

Eleven-year-old Dick with the family dog, five-year-old Diana, and seven-year-old Kathleen in front of the Huron Island keeper's house in 1941

Dick and his sisters loved the summer months when they all could live with their father at the lighthouse. Keeper Campbell tried to get ashore once a week during the school year, but the weather often prevented him from making the trip. So the family really looked forward to joining him once school was out, even though secluded Huron Island was desolate. "My mother constantly worried about us children climbing on those sharp rocks," says Dick. "Some areas of the small island were strictly off-limits because they were not safe. There were some sheer drop-offs into the lake." Photograph courtesy of the Campbell family

The work is there, and you do it. It was just natural. Everything was to be clean and dust free. Have you ever lived with a wood or coal stove? Can you imagine just the dusting job that had to be kept up living with a wood cookstove and a coal heating stove?

"Convenience was not part of our life," says Dick. "I first went to school in 1936, when we lived on Grassy Island, and my sisters and I had to be rowed across Detroit River to the school in Wyandotte, Michigan. Sometimes my dad would have to get out and push the skiff across the cold, slippery ice and then row the rest of the way. He not only had to work the light on Grassy Island, but also he serviced the many navigation buoys and range lights on the river. Acetylene gas cylinders had to be replaced often and lamps relit. My mother was not impressed when she first saw Grassy Island Light Station—there were us kids and a small lighthouse and no modern conveniences.

"If you went ashore to get mail, you also got food. And you picked up groceries for the other families on the island," Dick recalls. "We would have fresh meat for two days or so, and otherwise we ate fish from the lake. We fished, using our own nets, and sold to boats coming by the island. We'd signal to come in and pick up, although we weren't supposed to do this. We had a good relation with the commercial fishermen, and this is one way I got involved with fishing. It was part of what I grew up with. When Dad was on Huron Island, he would trade fish for empty lard kegs at the A&P store in L'Anse. During November and December when fish were spawning, he and the other lighthouse personnel would catch and salt the fish in the wooden kegs. It must have been a sight for the crew of the lighthouse tender when they came to pick up the keepers at the end of the season: lonesome men, baggage, and fish!

"During winters my father didn't have much to do, but this changed when the coast guard took over," continues Dick. "The coast guard took rundown or abandoned lighthouses along the lakes and made them into lookout stations for fishermen. If he wasn't doing that, the coast guard found some little job for him. For instance, they formed 'ice patrols.' If someone went out on the ice and got in trouble, my dad was expected to go and help. When the lighthouse service was absorbed by the coast guard, my dad was an older man, and that didn't go over well with a service made up of mainly young men. The old light keepers were set in their ways, too," Dick remembers with a chuckle.

"I remember that we moved a lot between L'Anse and Baraga, and I'm told I missed many things because I grew up at a lighthouse," Dick says. "I remember, especially as kids on Huron Island, we had to make our own entertainment because the island was only about a mile long and a quarter mile wide. And when your home is a pile of rocks, there aren't many activities to get involved in. We engaged in what you call 'creative play!' It was pretty desolate. My mother was constantly worried about us children climbing on those sharp rocks, and there were some areas strictly off-limits because they were

Assistant Keeper John Campbell and Keeper Jim Collins with a WPA band member on Huron Island
During the Depression, the government hired musicians as a make-work project to keep the economy going, and one of the WPA bands toured the Upper Peninsula of Michigan. The band members gave a concert on Huron Island, and when Dick's dad transported them back to the mainland in the big lighthouse boat, he allowed Dick to be towed behind in the lighthouse row-boat. Somewhere along the way, Dick's boat broke loose. "I figured when they got to the dock, they'd look back and I'd be gone and they'd say, 'Well, I'll be darned, where is Dick?' Oh, they came back and fished me out of the lake, and when I got back to the lighthouse, I was met with big cheers and lots of attention," recalls Dick. Photograph courtesy of the Campbell family

not safe. Some areas were sheer drop-offs into the lake. Often to fill our time we fished and went out in the rowboat. There was no shallow water, and we all learned to swim there—I don't remember ever seeing a life jacket. Lake Superior is cold, but we dove in regularly anyway. Years later, when my mother told about living at a lighthouse, I often wondered what she really thought about this!

"One of the government work programs during the war years provided for bands that traveled around to different locations and played for folks," Dick continues. "One time the WPA band came to the island. What a treat! When the time came for my dad to take them back to the mainland, it would have overloaded the boat to put me into it. So they loaded the band up in the big boat and let me get in the lighthouse rowboat and tied me with a rope to tag along the back. Well the wind was blowing pretty good and somehow the rope came loose from the big boat. I was young and strong so I just put the oars in the locks and started rowing in the same direction as the big boat. I figured when they got to the dock, they'd notice I wasn't back there anymore and come and get me. I can see it now just as it was then. I thought, well they'll look back and I'll be gone and they'll say, 'Well, I'll be darned, where is Dick?' Oh, they came back and fished me out of the lake, and when I got back to the lighthouse, I was met with big cheers and lots of attention!"

Dick has especially vivid memories of the Old Mackinac Point Light Station, where his father served as the last keeper before it was shut down in 1958. "Old Mac had a fourth-order lens turned by a clockwork mechanism to make the one large bull's-eye flash out across the Straits of Mackinac for the large ships," says Dick. "Alongside the large bull's-eye was a series of smaller bull's-eyes that made a smooth, steady ring of light for the smaller home fishing boats. When Old Mackinac Point Lighthouse closed down, replaced by radar technology and the big bridge (if mariners couldn't see the bridge, it was assumed they should not be on the straits), the insides of the station were dumped like trash."

Dick remembers his dad just shaking his head when workers came to crate up the Fresnel lens, the lens he had spent hours upon hours of his life polishing. As they watched the historic lens taken apart to be sold for scrap, his dad talked with Dick about the history behind the French-designed lens, its beauty, its art, and its value as an old friend. He reminisced about having unscrewed each brass holder and thoroughly cleaning the lens section by section. It hurt to see it being dismantled by workers who had little knowledge of or interest in its history.

Fortunately some of the pieces of historic Old Mackinac Point Light Station have been saved. The brass dustpan his father had polished to perfection and dutifully filled with the dust he had cleaned off everything is part of the museum collection at the Old Mackinac Point Museum. And Dick has his father's uniform and cap as well as the brass oilcans his father filled each night and the small brass measures for daily keepers' jobs.

"Old Mackinac Point was a shore station where we could all live together all year-round," says Dick. "This was the longest time Dad served at one station—fourteen years! Life was much different at Old Mackinac Point because we were part of a community. I graduated from high school there and then entered the air force. I also married my high school sweetheart, Nancy Dagwell, whose father was the marine reporter. They lived just down the shore from the lighthouse.

"I remember working hard every Saturday for my dad at Old Mackinac Point Lighthouse," adds Dick. "It had a big two-family house with little insulation. It took lots of coal, burned 'hard' to keep that place warm. Other than helping move the coal when it was delivered, it was my job to haul out the ashes and clean the clinkers—pieces of charred coal–off the grates of the stoves. What a job."

After supervising the closing of Old Mackinac Point Light Station, Keeper Campbell and his family moved to Point Betsie Light Station in Frankfort, Michigan. Dick's father died in August 1963, four months before his retirement date, thirty-one years after joining the U.S. Lighthouse Service.

Like many other keepers' children, Dick lives near one of his childhood lighthouse homes. "Most of the family came back," Dick says, "and if they didn't, they wanted to be here. I know my heart has always been here near the lighthouses where I worked with my dad. After four years in the air force, I returned to Mackinaw City to work for the Michigan State Ferries."

Dick also worked for the Mackinac Bridge Authority. "My job was inspecting the piers of the framework of the bridge, and this came from my work on tugs and barges on the lakes. When a ship hit the bridge, I inspected the damage. And it all goes back to lighthouses–experience comes with seeing and doing."

Also like many other keepers' children raised in relative isolation with little peer contact, Dick is a loner. He has learned to work for his own cause and not worry about what other people do. For example, Dick has long worked with American Indians to help regain their fishing rights. "I am a member of the Sault Ste. Marie Tribe of Chippewas and am very proud of my heritage," he explains. "My father and especially my grandmother would be very happy to see the outcome of the treaty decisions granted us to keep whitefish fishing alive within Native American culture. I remain active at tribal gatherings. As I grew up, I learned so much of the elders' ways from my father and grandmother."

Dick keeps his family's Native American heritage alive by practicing traditional customs such as burning sage and cedar as a ritual of blessing and sprinkling tobacco, something from the earth, into the lake in exchange for fish taken for nourishment.

Dick goes to Arizona at Christmastime every year to be with his son. Just as Dick did many decades ago, his son now watches for his father to arrive for the holidays.

FAMILY RECIPES

Dick shares his childhood recipe for ice cream, which he says his family made during summers at Huron Island. The Campbells had a kerosene-powered refrigerator the last two years they lived on Huron Island, but most perishables were kept chilled in the cold Lake Superior waters, wrapped in a gunnysack tied securely to a rock on shore. Perhaps Dick was only dreaming of making ice cream while they were there in the 1930s.

DICK CAMPBELL'S CHILDHOOD RECIPE FOR ICE CREAM

1 can cold milk	1 cup sugar
1 egg 10 minutes	A little vanilla
in refrigerator	A pinch of salt

Mix all together well. Put in freezer to harden.

DEVIL'S FOOD CAKE

Mrs. Collins, the principal keeper's wife, often made this cake in the keeper's kitchen on Huron Island.

1 cup sugar	1 egg, well-beaten
3/4 cup cocoa	1 cup milk

Combine sugar and cocoa. Add well-beaten egg; add milk. Cook in double boiler until thick and smooth. Let cool.

3/4 cup shortening	1 teaspoon baking soda
1 cup sugar	1/8 teaspoon salt
2 eggs, well-beaten	1/2 cup sour milk
2 cups cake flour	1 teaspoon vanilla

Cream shortening and sugar. Add eggs; beat thoroughly. Sift flour, measure, and sift with baking soda and salt. Add dry ingredients alternately with sour milk and vanilla to the first mixture; blend thoroughly but lightly. Allow to stand a few minutes. Pour into well-oiled cake pans. Bake at 350° until straw comes out clean. Let cool on cake rack.

HURON ISLAND LIGHT STATION is 5 miles off the eastern shore of the Keweenaw Peninsula in Michigan's Upper Peninsula. Unfortunately strong currents and winds prohibit public access to the island, which is owned by the U.S. Coast Guard.

OLD MACKINAC POINT LIGHT STATION can be easily seen from the I-75 bridge across the Straits of Mackinac that connects Upper and Lower Michigan. Take exit 336 off I-75, follow Nicolet Avenue through Mackinaw City, and turn right onto Huron Avenue. The lighthouse is about two blocks down in a park on the lefthand side of the street. The lighthouse is open seasonally from early May until early October. For more details on exhibits and tower tours led by a costumed interpreter, call 231/436-8705. The Great Lakes Lighthouse Keepers Association (GLLKA) operates a gift shop across the street from the lighthouse. Headquartered in the same building, GLLKA answers questions year-round about Great Lakes Lighthouses.

GRASSY ISLAND is at the mouth of the Detroit River where it flows into Lake Erie. Unfortunately the lighthouse is no longer standing.

POINT BETSIE LIGHT STATION was among the last light stations to be automated. Resident keepers operated the light until 1983. In 2004, the lighthouse was transferred to Benzie County and is managed and maintained by a non-profit group, The Friends of Point Betsie Lighthouse, which has restored and opened the light to the public. It has become a popular visitor destination as well as a lovely spot for weddings. Call 231/352-7666.

Croatan River Light, North Carolina

The screwpile-style Croatan River Light warned ships to steer clear of the shoals at the north end of Croatan Sound, between the Outer Banks and the North Carolina mainland. Built soon after the Civil War to replace lightships that tended to break loose from their anchors, North Carolina's river lights provided the keeper—or the keeper and his assistant—about 1,000 square feet of living space. At each light, the tower rose through the roof of the one- or two-story dwelling on the platform supported about 12 feet above the water by five steel pilings that were "screwed" into the soft, muddy bottom of the river or sound. All of North Carolina's river and sound lights have disappeared except Roanoke River Light, which has been moved to Colonial Park on the Edenton waterfront. At the time of this printing, the lighthouse is undergoing restoration and will be open to the public in the near future. For more information, call the Edenton Historical Commission at 252/482-7800. Photograph courtesy of the U.S. Coast Guard

CROATAN & LONG SHOAL
LIFE AT A RIVER LIGHT

Thomas Hardy Baum became first assistant keeper at Cape Hatteras Light Station in 1905. During his lifelong career with the U.S. Lighthouse Service, Keeper Baum served several of the river lights that were built on inland waters of the Pamlico, Croatan, and Albemarle Sounds during the years just following the Civil War. By 1891 about sixteen river lights provided more reliable navigational aid than lightship vessels. Although they were invaluable safety markers, lightships tended to break loose from their anchors and wreak havoc for mariners in more ways than one. The river lights were called "screwpile" lighthouses because they had threaded metal caps to "screw" the pilings deep into the soft, muddy bottoms of sounds and rivers.

For decades navigators felt their way along the dark inland waterways using the river lighthouses much as a priest uses rosary beads as a trusted source of guidance and comfort. But after paved highways replaced the traditional waterways, shipping dwindled on North Carolina's rivers and sounds, eliminating the need for the screwpile lights. The river lights that once sparkled like diamonds in the night across the Outer Banks and the North Carolina mainland disappeared. Only one, which has been moved to private property, survives to date, and memories about these historic lights are just as rare as the lights themselves.

Wayland Baum, the son of Keeper Thomas Hardy Baum, is one of the few living witnesses to everyday life at a river light. Following in his father's footsteps, Wayland worked for the U.S. Lighthouse Service, first, on the side-paddle steamer tender Holly and later as a substitute keeper at Long Shoal River Light and other lighthouses. With warmth and humor, he shares his memories of living and working at a screwpile lighthouse.

Wayland Baum was born in 1904 in Wanchese, just across the sound from where his mother, Lillie C. Miller, was born and raised in Buxton, North Carolina. For years his family lived in Baumtown, around Baumtown Creek, right off Mann's Harbor, where all the Baums lived, according to Wayland. His first memories are sensations of going up and down, around and around, up and down, around and around.

"When my mother was sickly with an attack of epilepsy and could not take care of me, my daddy would tote me and a five-gallon brass can of kerosene up and down the Cape Hat'ress Lighthouse when he was first assistant keeper." There, atop the tall lighthouse, father and young son stood watch together until Lillie felt better.

Wayland can still picture his father wind the clockwork mechanism that rotated the first-order Fresnel lens at Cape Hatteras. "It worked a lot like the fogbell worked on the river lights with heavy weights," Wayland says. "They had to be wound about every thirty minutes. On screwpile lighthouses, the foghorn was operated by a motor."

Horizon and water become one in heavy fog. The familiar landmark on the shore takes on new identity, and as you move along, the fog creates a very small, enclosed world where the way to your destination becomes illusive. A lifelong fisherman, Wayland testifies to the importance of the screwpile river lights. "They were the only way I could get my bearings when fog or bad weather set in. If I was out oystering and it was foggy, I would stop my boat's engine and listen for the foghorn from the river light to get my location from Roanoke Island. You didn't want to lose your way out there in the maze of passages that all looked the same. A man could disappear for days if he couldn't tell where he was. The river lights and fogbells or foghorns were real important. I remember Roanoke Marshes had a foghorn, but it was changed to a bell after there wasn't anybody there [after it was automated about 1950] to operate the engine.

"My daddy was at Cape Hat'ress, Long Shoal, and Tangier Island," says Wayland.

"He retired from the screwpile light at Caroon's Point, also known as Croatan River Light," right off Marshoes Creek on Croatan Sound." As a child Wayland helped his dad at the river lights, and as a man he

The moon rising behind the fourth-order Fresnel lens at Hooper Strait Light Station in Maryland

Wayland Baum grew up watching and helping his father tend fourth-order Fresnel lenses, like this one, at several of North Carolina's river lighthouses. Unfortunately all but one of North Carolina's river lights have disappeared.

Long Shoal River Light, North Carolina

The U.S. Lighthouse Service did not allow wives and children to live at river lights, but most ignored the rule—and hid in the wood closet when the lighthouse inspectors came around. About 1915 when Keeper Baum was serving Long Shoal River Light, young Wayland lost his balance and fell through the rods and latchings connecting the supporting screwpiles. "It's a wonder I didn't get killed," Wayland says, with a look of disbelief still today. Some twenty years later, Wayland returned to Long Shoal with his wife, Vivian, as a substitute keeper. After living through a rough storm, Vivian swore she would never set foot on a river light again. "And she didn't," Wayland says with finality. Photograph courtesy of the U.S. Coast Guard

served as a substitute keeper at Long Shoal River Light.

He recalls that the keeper's boat was often hung on two iron davits, suspended by two sets of falls. It was raised and lowered by a hand-wound wench. "I kept the davits painted real good to keep them from rusting," Wayland remembers. "This was the big boat—a smaller 'hull' boat may have been kept below on a platform. Oil and other supplies as well as equipment was stored outside under the platform, but still above the

Keeper Thomas Hardy Baum and his wife, Lillie C. Miller Baum, on the steps of the double keepers' house at Cape Hatteras in 1905

Wayland's father, Thomas Hardy Baum, began his lighthouse service career in 1905 as first assistant keeper at Cape Hatteras Light Station. "I remember the feelings of going up and down and around and around while Daddy carried me up and down the steps with him in the Hat'ress Lighthouse," Wayland clearly recalls. "I guess I knew I always wanted to be a lighthouse keeper too." His mother suffered from epilepsy, and Wayland's father often took care of him when she was not feeling well. Notice Lillie's pocketwatch tucked into the belt around her tiny waist. Photograph courtesy of Faye Baum White

water level. A fogbell hung just above the first floor outside a dormer, which provided a little bit of protection from the elements. Mariners depended on the bell's warning as much as seeing the screwpile itself during the day in addition to the light's beam at night." Like all lighthouse keepers, Wayland and his father were no strangers to second and third work shifts.

Although the water level under a river light usually did not vary a great deal, the tides and currents running under the water's surface were deceptively muscular. And storms brought both high water and high wind. Wayland remembers a wind stronger than 100 miles per hour that kept blowing out the Croatan River Light. "I relit that light seven times that night. Of course you couldn't see fifty feet in the storm, but I still relit the light seven times.

"The wick was round, made of cotton, about two inches around," says Wayland. "To prepare the light, I'd carry the oil reservoir part of the lamp down to the second level where the kerosene was stored. We had a stand where we could set the oil filling part, fill and clean it, and then take it back up to the lantern room and put the two-foot-tall glass chimney on it. About thirty minutes before sundown, I'd light the wick and let it burn to a certain level where I knew it wouldn't run up [burn too high] on me. If it run up on me, it would smoke up the chimney of the lamp and have to be cleaned and start all over. If I didn't watch the light so it burned just right, it'd smoke up the entire lantern room. And then I'd have to scrub the whole room. What a scrubbing job! It took hours to get it clean again.

"All parts of the lamp and filling cans were made of brass and had to be kept shiny," he explains. "We had two kinds of polishing materials. One was a paste, used when tough cleanup jobs needed to be done and things were real dingy. And we had another, dry 'Sal Soda' scrubbing powder, for quick cleanups.

"To clean the lamp and all the glass, including the prisms of the Fresnel lens, we'd use newspapers. I'd ball up the paper over and over until it was nice and soft. Then I'd polish the glass and everything with it. While Daddy was in the old lighthouse service, the government would give him chamois cloth to clean with. But he would save that for special cleanings like the prisms and use newspaper or any old cloths he could find to clean the brass in between [times of cleaning]. When I was keeper, I'd take the softened newsprint and rub and rub and then take a cloth, anything soft I could find, and rub and rub more until the prisms and other glass were real clean and pretty."

Wayland explains that shifts of three men, two on duty at all times, were stationed at each river light. When one man returned from time off on the mainland, one man would have his things packed and hop on board to go home. Two boats were kept at each river light at all times. "One was a powerboat," says Wayland, "and one was a little old regular sailboat. If a man wanted to get off real bad before the third man returned, he'd have to take the sailboat. It was quite a row sometimes to the mainland. My daddy had his own powerboat at all times when he was keeper. That way he could use it for fishing. It got us food and some extra money when needed. Keepers often kept a dropnet at the lighthouse for fishing—mostly just personal. The government didn't mind.

"The oil was kept in big, wide closets along with wood and paint," Wayland continued. "There were bedrooms on either end of Long Shoal and Croatan Light. Steps led up into the center hallway, and you entered the closets from the bedroom areas."

The keepers kept "nonregulation" things in those closets sometimes. For instance, families were not supposed to stay at the lighthouse, and when the inspector came to do his routine check, all he wanted to see was the light in good order and the men hard at work. "We could see the old steamer coming five or six miles away with the inspector's flag flying. We could see all this black smoke coming our way! And if we were there Daddy would tell us to hide. Yes, even my mother had to hide in that dark wood closet on the second level. We'd hide behind the wood pile in the closet and couldn't cough or sneeze. We had to be absolutely quiet. And years later when I was keeper and my wife, Vivian, was there, the same would happen.

"Yes, of course the inspector could see signs of a wife or children. As far as we knew, he could tell … he could tell. But the inspector was 'good folks.' He wouldn't say anything if all was in good order. He knew life was hard and lonely on these river lights. He knew if a good job was being done for the lighthouse service. He understood what was going on."

Sometimes though it wasn't the inspector's boat. "Sometimes it was just an old steam tug and we'd get fooled. But we ran the drill anyway," laughs Wayland.

The privy at a river light "hung off" one side of the platform. Wayland says, "At Croatan the privy was on the north side, and at Long Shoal it was on south side—I know because I knew these lights all my life. I remember visiting Keepers Charlie Pugh and Oscar Daniels at Roanoke Marshes Light very well and visiting the privy!" Wayland adds that local fishermen used to laugh about approaching a river light and being able to tell if the keeper was "busy."

Wayland emphasizes that life was spartan as well as dangerous at the river lights. The keepers would make periodic trips to the mainland, 5 or so miles away to get provisions. Ice was a rare commodity, and whatever was brought to the lighthouse had

to keep for several days. There was a shelf below the platform to keep potatoes, watermelons, and sometimes even live chickens. The chickens were kept in a crate, and when the keeper wanted chicken for dinner, someone would just

Keeper Thomas Hardy Baum and Wayland about 1915

"There weren't any cameras on the Outer Banks that I can recall before I was grown," Wayland says to explain why he has so few childhood photographs. Families hired professionals to take keepsake pictures, like this one taken in a studio in Norfolk, Virginia. Photograph courtesy of Willie Hearne Mann

open the trapdoor of the platform, descend the steel ladder, and grab a chicken.

Wayland vividly remembers one particular time when he was sent to get something from the storage area at Long Shoal River Light. His father had brought back a piece of beef from the mainland "Daddy said one day, 'Wayland, go get a piece of meat for supper.' I remember going down through the trapdoor with a pan in one hand and a knife in the other. Somehow, I don't know how, I lost my balance on the first step of the ladder and fell right over backward, clean through all the wires and cross pilings and steel rods all the way to the water—I never touched a one. I went under in the cold water of the sound and was stunned. I came up gasping for air, scared to death. I had lost the pan and knife, and I was so scared. I grabbed onto one of the big old rods just above the water a little ways and hung on for dear life. I was locked on with my feet and legs and arms wrapped around the steel wire like a scared possum! Daddy didn't know whether to be glad or sad. If I'd hit one of those steel rods on the way down, it'd have killed me."

Some of the steel rods of Long Shoal River Light are still standing. About 1955 the coast guard tore down the rest of the lighthouse and put an automated light on a platform on the rods. "The screwpile rods still stand in some part, but it's a shame all the lights as they were have been lost," notes Wayland.

Wayland Baum, quite the fashionable young man, about 1925
"I bought this Model T truck from Ignatius Scarborough, who built a speedboat for my daddy. We called it the 'Green Lizard,' and the truck part was homemade," Wayland tells with a proud grin. "You had to crank it just fast enough to start the generator—it had no bat'ry." Photograph courtesy of the Baum family

When he grew up Wayland joined the U.S. Lighthouse Service and worked on the tender *Holly*, which serviced buoys all through the Chesapeake Bay and down the North Carolina coast. "They had outside tenders for the lightships and inside tenders for buoys and river lights on the sounds. The old *Holly* was a side-paddle tender," Wayland explains. "Once in a while we had the inspector to take around to all the lights in the district for inspections. We were always glad of that because when the inspector was on board, we didn't have to deliver wood and coal and kerosene. We kindly had a

Keeper Thomas Hardy Baum enjoying a rare vacation about 1925

"My daddy was at Cape Hat'ress, Long Shoal, and Tangier Island," says Wayland. "He retired from the screwpile light at Caroon's Point, also known as Croatan River Light." Like all river light keepers, Thomas Baum was on call almost twenty-four hours a day, seven days a week. River light keepers were responsible for maintaining all of the navigational aids in the area, including post lanterns, which housed small Fresnel-type lenses and oil-fueled lamps that burned continuously for three to eight days. In addition to making routine rounds to refill the oil reservoirs, keepers were often called out at night to repair or refuel a post lantern that had gone out. More than a few keepers drowned tending these small but essential lights. Photograph courtesy of the Baum family

cinch when he was on there. Otherwise when we delivered coal and wood, we'd have to bag up to sixty tons of coal on the front deck into two-hundred-pound bags.

"Coming in from the sound side, we'd lighter the load onto smaller skiffs and get as close to the dock as possible. Then we'd have to carry it on our backs in water up to our knees—no, sometimes up to our waist—the rest of the way to shore. When we returned to the tender we'd have to scrub all that coal dust off the boat and make the paint shine as white as if the coal had never been there. Even if we were headed back to Portsmouth to get another load of coal to deliver to another lighthouse, we'd still have to scrub and scrub to get that tender's white paint clean again on the inside. It didn't make a lot of sense to us, but the crew followed orders from the captain, who got his orders from the lighthouse service."

The crew was made up of the captain of the tender, two quartermasters, two mates, and six sailors. "I was a sailor," says Wayland, "and I did all the totin' and scrubbin'!"

The following year, about 1923, found Wayland on a "seatug" that did all sorts of towing from Charleston, South Carolina, to the coast of Maine. The tug towed barges burdened with loads of lumber from the rich ports of the East Coast to other ports of need. Wayland had earned his AB "able-bodied" seaman ticket, which meant $5 extra pay each month. If a man was just an "ordinary," he got $50 a month, while an AB seaman earned a prized $55 a month. The quartermaster earned $75 a month, a mate got about $125 a month, and the captain earned a respected $225 to $250 a month.

Wayland's father had enjoyed a lifelong career as a lightkeeper, and Wayland too desired to serve. His first application was turned down, unfairly he feels. "The people who promised me a recommendation didn't follow through," Wayland says with candor. Wayland continued to correspond with a U.S. Lighthouse Service administrator to obtain a reconsideration, and his appointment as a substitute keeper came only after great effort on his part to convince the lighthouse service that he was the man they needed. Disappointed that he had not been given a full-time position, Wayland reluctantly accepted his first duty at Turkey Point, Maryland, where he served with the same dignity and competence his father had shown.

"When I was a keeper, one of the main duties on our watch was to keep the books [logs]. It was real important that the books were kept to the inspector's approval. It was one of the difficult parts of taking time off. Whoever was in charge had to make sure those books were kept right."

Wayland continued to receive assignments as a substitute keeper and served at Bodie Island Light Station as well as Croatan and Long Shoal River Lights. "When I was stationed at Long Shoal, Vivian and I hadn't been married long. The lighthouse was old [built in 1867] and not as strong as others. It didn't have

Wayland as a "young man"
Wayland says, "This is when I was a young man, in about my midsixties. Since the lighthouse service didn't give me a full-time keeper's job for a long time, I survived mainly as a fisherman. My skin was as tough as leather." Photograph courtesy of the Baum family

stabilizing stringers on the north and south sides of the building, so it rocked a lot worse than the light at Croatan. A storm blew up and the rocking chair in the living room was just a-swayin'!

"One time on the Croatan Light," he continues, "a bad storm with hundred-mile-per-hour winds came up. The building had a tin roof. It kept making so much noise that we couldn't hear each other unless we got right up in each other's face and yelled. It was so scary because we didn't know how much worse it would get. Vivian said, 'If I get my feet on dry land again, I'll never set my foot on another river lighthouse again.' And she didn't!"

Despite Vivian's refusal to join him on the river, Wayland continued to serve as a substitute keeper. "Men were given up to thirty days of leave each year. I would be expected to fill in whenever and wherever I was needed. Though I was kept busy with lighthouse duty, I kept my fishing business going," he notes.

Wayland worked hard for the lighthouse service and finally received a full-time keeper's appointment at Turkey Point, Maryland. But realizing that he still had hard feelings from years of waiting, he eventually resigned from the service. "A friend and I bought a stand of gill nets and went shad fishing, the main income for Dare County for a long, long time. But I never lost my respect for the lights. They brought me home many a time. No, I'd have never made it without the lights," Wayland says.

FAMILY RECIPE

"Mother was sickly most of the time and Dad had to do most of the cooking. I remember that Dad could make the best beef roast and gravy anywhere ... he had a real knack to make it turn out real good. He used a wood stove, better than any modern one, that had a thermometer on the outside. He would bake sweet potatoes and biscuits, too.

CLABBER BISCUITS

Mrs. Genie Williams of Manteo, one of the finest cooks in North Carolina, advised Wayland on this recipe. Genie says, "I didn't like clabber biscuits when I was young, so my mother used sweet milk and made me a

*batch of those. She had her own cow and would set the milk in bowls, allow-
ing the cream to come to the top. If the milk was allowed to sit, it would sour
and get firm, and that's where clabber came from.*"

¼ cup lard, Crisco, or butter
2 cups self-rising flour
1 cup buttermilk (clabber)
Large pinch (¼ teaspoon) baking soda
1 teaspoon sugar

*Cut lard into flour until mixture looks like coarse cornmeal. Blend in butter-
milk, baking soda, and sugar. Knead lightly, but don't over knead—the more
biscuit dough is kneaded, the tougher it becomes. Roll out dough or flatten it
with your hands to about ¾-inch thickness. Cut biscuits with a glass or cutter, and place on baking sheet.*

*Set the biscuits in a warm place for about 30 minutes, and let them "grow."
Bake in hot oven (400° to 450°) for 10-12 minutes. Rub the tops with butter
and put back in oven for 1 more minute to finish browning.*

LONG SHOAL RIVER LIGHT, CROATAN RIVER LIGHT (also called
CAROON'S POINT RIVER LIGHT), and the rest of North Carolina's river
and sound lights are now gone except ROANOKE RIVER LIGHT, which has
been relocated to the historic waterfront in Edenton, NC. For more information call
the Historic Edenton State Historic Sites at 252/482-2637.

Pigeon Point Light Station,
California

POINT REYES PIGEON POINT

GROWING UP IN TWO WORLDS

Keeper Gerhard Jaehne grew up to be a rider of horses, waves, and light beams. As a teenager in the early 1900s, Gerhard paid little attention to his father's wishes to work in his toy factory on the Oder River in Germany. He longed to be a cowboy and seaman, and he knew he could do both if he would only venture upon the sea to America–so he did. The industrious fourteen-year-old served on merchant sailing ships, learning Italian and English on the way. Gerhard returned to Germany to attend navigation school but soon after graduation became an officer on a steamship headed for New York. From there he made a trail for Montana, gained his U.S. citizenship, and worked a ranch–until his love of the sea led him to the U.S. Lighthouse Service. Keeper Jaehne served at a number of light stations before his retirement in 1952, including Mile Rocks, St. George Reef, Point Reyes, Pigeon Point, and Oakland Harbor. His distinguished service earned him the coveted Gallatin Award, the highest award that can be given to a federal civilian employee.

Keeper Jaehne and his wife, Etta, had four children: Carl, Alice, Claude, and Herman. Alice and Herman share their memories of growing up at Point Reyes and Pigeon Point. "Every day was a whole new experience," starts Alice. "And Christmas generally was a Hershey candy bar wrapped up real pretty," Herman chimes in. Sister and brother agree that theirs was the best childhood anyone could have.

Between 1917 and 1921 in a log cabin in the wilderness of Montana, four children were born to Gerhard Jaehne and Etta Roberts Jaehne, a teacher from Iowa who had married the would-be cowboy from Germany. Surrounded by his family and horses, Gerhard at first thought he had everything he ever wanted, but before long he realized something was missing–the sound of the sea.

So he signed on with the U.S. Lighthouse Service, took leave of his wife and children, and journeyed to his first assignment at Mile Rocks in San Francisco Bay. His second assignment, at St. George Reef–where few men dared serve, tested his fortitude and career intentions. Located 6 miles off the northern California coast on Dragon Reef, St. George Reef Light Station endures wicked waves that not only endlessly pound the tower but also destroy many a keeper's plans to stay in the lighthouse service. But stay he did, and Gerhard continued his sterling career as principal keeper at Point Reyes Lighthouse just north of San Francisco.

Gerhard received his first reward from his new job in 1923. It arrived on a train from Montana in the form of Etta, six-year-old Carl, four-year-old Alice, three-year-old Claude, and two-year-old Herman. Little Herm had cried a lot of the way, but he soon began wearing a perpetual smile. It was the beginning of eight years of great adventures for the Jaehne kids.

Herman begins, "My strongest memory of Point Reyes is the ocean. I've always loved the ocean. I remember the dangerous point of rounding the lighthouse for the boats. The Italians had the best ones, the Monterey clipper boats–beautiful boats, that were always painted blue and white. They were only 28-footers but could ride the waves with amazing success. I remember watching them round Point Reyes and literally being buried by the waves, but they just popped up. And they just had a one-cylinder engine that went 'Plunk … Plunk'–they sounded as if they were about to die, but they just kept going! When I was nine or ten years old, I loved to go down to Drake's Bay and go out with them fishing for salmon. They even let

Keeper Gerhard Jaehne at Point Reyes in 1925

Frequent thick fog, high winds, and ship-splitting rocks made Point Reyes a mariner's nightmare–and a keeper's challenge. The light station's foghorn frequently sounded round the clock, and blustery winds often gusted over a hundred miles an hour. Wearing a heavy woolen peacoat over his U.S. Lighthouse Service uniform to block out the penetrating natural elements, Keeper Gerhard often stood watch on the catwalk, keeping a sharp eye out for ships in trouble. Photograph courtesy of the Jaehne family

Point Reyes Light Station, California
Many ships, large and small, met disaster at Point Reyes. Standing atop the sheer 300-foot cliff, the lighthouse warned mariners not to try to land on the 10-mile inhospitable peninsula that deceptively looks like an island harbor.

me smoke their pipes. The skipper would tie the pipe around my neck so I wouldn't drop it overboard. I just loved that."

"We would go down to the bay where the fishermen came in to eat," sister Alice continues. "We'd sit at long tables and benches and get fed like the fishermen. We'd eat spaghetti and French bread."

All four Jaehne kids went to school about a mile and a half away at a dairy ranch

Keeper Gerhard Jaehne polishing the prisms of the first-order Fresnel lens in the lantern room of Point Reyes Lighthouse about 1925

Point Reyes Lighthouse has marked the way to San Francisco Bay for more than one and a quarter centuries, and many a keeper and his helpers—including his children—have polished the prisms and windows of the lantern room. "There was always something to clean," says Herman Jaehne. Photograph courtesy of the Jaehne family

owned by the Mendoza family. Sometimes the kids rode Billy the horse to school. "I think he was first brought to us because one of the assistant's children had polio and had to wear a brace and couldn't get around real well. But we got to ride him too. That horse was so gentle that if one of us kids fell off, he'd just stand there until we got back on. We'd ride him to the second dairy ranch, and they'd take care of him during the day, and we'd ride him back home," Herman explains in his casual manner. "Mother also could hook him up to a buggy and go to the ranch and pick up our mail—they wouldn't deliver any farther than that."

The school had ten students—the four Jaehnes, three of the assistant keepers' children—Melba and Lorraine Vradenburg and one of the Conklin children, two sons from the coast guard family from the lifeboat station in Drake's Bay—Buddy and Sonny Underhill, and a boy from a family that lived on the Mendoza Ranch. The teacher, Fannie Calvert, boarded at the ranch. Herman and a friend made up the fifth grade, while Alice alone composed the sixth. "We didn't have a playground unless we figured out how to keep the cows out of the way," Herman grins.

The children got their textbooks and then did most of their learning on their own—including how to get home without inciting the resident bull. Alice grimaces, "One day when we went across the field to go home we heard snorting behind us, and oh my, there was a bull charging at us! The boys ran across the field and scooted under the fence. But I panicked and got caught on the wire. I still have a scar that runs from my knee clear up my thigh. I remember the boys getting me home and Mother and Dad opening the cut and pouring iodine on it. Oh, how I remember how I screamed and cried! But there were no stitches and no infection. Amazing.

"There was a hill just down from the school, and one time my three brothers made a makeshift wagon out of a plank and two big wheels. Now Mother and Daddy always told us, 'Whatever you do, don't roll down that hill!' And of course Carl and Claude did, and Claude broke his collarbone. Anything they told Claude not to do, he did. They took him to the hospital in San Rafael, but in those days around 1930, bones weren't set. The doctor put a wooden cross on his back and strapped his arm to his chest."

"Claude was the boldest," Herman recalls. "If there was trouble to be found, Claude would find it. He fell off the cliff near our house and luckily landed on a ledge—or he'd have gone 600 feet clear down to the Pacific! A real little bulldozer, he was. But he always took care of me.

"In the winter we would trap skunks and 'coons on the way to school. We could get one dollar for a skunk skin and three for a 'coon. Oh, yeah, the skunks got us sometimes—we'd have to change clothes outside before going in the house," Herman chuckles.

Alice adds, "I had to do most of the washing with Mother. We had running water at

Point Reyes, and the washroom was down below the keeper's house—we had washtubs and a wringer washer. We hung the clothes right on the edge of a cliff—it was straight down!"

"I helped Mother with other

Alice Jaehne at Point Reyes in 1926
Alice Jaehne posed outside the keeper's house on a cliff above the lighthouse. There are more than 400 steps between the keeper's house, or quarters, and the tower below. In addition to blinding fog, blustery winds capable of gusting up to 100 miles per hour frequently assaulted Point Reyes. Even the average 25- to 45-mile-per-hour winds made the trek up the steps more physically challenging. Photograph courtesy of the Jaehne family

121

The keeper's house at Point Reyes Light Station

This is one of the few light stations where the keeper's house towered over the lighthouse. "There were 638 steps from the foghorn to the keeper's house," Herman remembers. "Below the water tank was a small framework with weather gauges," adds Alice. At one time, the four Jaehne children, all under the age of six, lived and played in and around this house perched precariously on the rocks. The house no longer stands at Point Reyes Light Station, but visitors can still walk down the steps to the lighthouse—unless the winds are too strong. Photograph courtesy of the Jaehne family

jobs like doing dishes too," she continues. "At Point Reyes the kitchen window was on the back of the house, almost flush with the cliff that went straight down several hundred feet into rough ocean. One time I had just put the pots and pans in the open window above the sink. The boys came barreling in the front door, the wind whipped right through the house, and out the window went the pots and pans. We heard them CRASH! BANG! down the cliffs!"

"North Beach," Herman picks up, "was a ten-mile beach that ran from Point Reyes to Tomales Bay. The prevailing winds were from the north so everything would drift into that beach—even notes in bottles. For the most part they said, 'This is the last of the whiskey on board.'

"Often San Francisco fishing boats came out to the point. The crews didn't realize how rough the area could be and ended up losing their boats. I don't remember any casualties, just lots of disappointment," Herman analyzes.

The foghorn at Point Reyes usually blasted more than 2,000 hours a year—which adds up to about one day in three that it sounded around the clock. In addition to fog, blustery winds capable of gusting to more than 100 miles per hour often assaulted Point Reyes. Even in the normal 25- to 45-mile per hour winds, anyone climbing up or down the 400-plus steps from the keeper's house to the lighthouse and the many more steps from there down to the foghorn building had better hang onto his hat. Keeper Jaehne, Etta, and their four children risked being blown away day in and day out—it was just part of living and working at Point Reyes.

Incandescent oil vapor lamp (IOV) at Point Reyes
Before electricity, an incandescent oil vapor lamp provided the light source for the Fresnel lens at Point Reyes. This complicated lamp system, which operated like a modern Coleman lamp, heated the kerosene fuel so it vaporized before it ignited, yielding a brighter light. Photograph courtesy of the Jaehne family

"One time a 16-foot dory came in and the coast guard brought it to us kids at Drake's Bay," says Herman. Big fishing companies out of San Francisco would bring barges up into the bay and process the fish right there. The three of us boys would go out there in our dory all the time; everybody knew us. In the winter they'd give us fish to take home."

Medical supplies as well as most provisions such as flour, salt, and sugar came by lighthouse tender. "But most of our vegetables were canned, and we ate mostly fish," Herman explains.

Alice picks up on the subject, "We just didn't run to the store."

"Yeah," Herman smiles, "the store was twenty-five miles away. Every trip by car meant at least six flat tires. Dad would have to put in a new tube, and away we went—'til the next flat tire."

"We had wonderful Dungeness crab," Alice says. "Mother would get big pots boiling on our coal cooking stove. The huge crabs would be crawling everywhere on the kitchen floor! They were the best eating."

Turning to Alice, Herman asks, "Remember the turkey? One Thanksgiving Dad got a turkey and put it in some sort of pen he built." Either Gerhard Jaehne was less

Claude, Carl, and Alice at Point Reyes in 1926
For this picture, Alice and two of her brothers perched on one of the few sandy spots at Point Reyes Light Station. Photograph courtesy of the Jaehne family

talented as a carpenter than as a keeper, parent, or artist—or the turkey had been trained by Houdini. "Somehow that turkey got out. Everyone for miles, the farmers and coast-guardsmen, everybody was looking for it. We never found that 'dam turkey!"

The Jaehnes recall seeing the lighthouse tender often, an advantage to being stationed so close to the port of San Francisco. Herman says their neighboring farmers came with their horses and carts to help carry supplies from the landing dock to the light station. Sometimes the tender delivered a "special" visitor—the U.S. Lighthouse Service Inspector.

Alice says, "The inspector's visit was always telegraphed ahead to the keepers. Daddy would say to get all ready and everything shined. We did a lot of polishing brass, remember Herm?" Alice glances at her brother.

The inspectors' visits weren't the only things that brought a frenzy of activity at Point Reyes. "Once," says Alice, "there was a real bad electrical storm. The staircase from the living room was glassed in—I remember Dad had lots of plants in there. The lightning came right through the glass and knocked out Herman's crystal radio. I remember the pieces came flying down the stairs—it just broke it into a million pieces. It also broke the flagpole at the cistern," Alice finishes.

It would have been enough for any mother to raise four close-together, full-of-life youngsters, but Etta did it at a lighthouse perched on rocky cliffs where heavy fog, high winds, and horrendous storms were the norm. "Our mother was sweet," states Alice.

"She was so easy. Nothing bothered Mother," Herman adds warmly. "It's a wonder we survived! The whole place was rock with nothing but rough seas all around. It was no playground for young children. Mother must have been scared to death most of the time that one of us would get hurt. But we made it. There were 432 steps down to the lighthouse back then with no landings to stop and rest. On the entire station one wrong step meant the end," he adds as he flips through the family album.

Looking at the picture of the principal keeper's house atop the incline of Point Reyes, Alice points out the water tank. "Below the tank was a small framework with weather gauges for wind velocity and direction and barometric pressure and such," Alice says.

"Mother earned twenty-five dollars a month for reporting every day to the U.S. Department of Agriculture in San Francisco. She called them on a magneto, hand-crank telephone," concludes Herman.

Claude Jaehne in a double exposure taken by Irving Conklin at Point Reyes about 1930
Irving Conklin took this photograph when he was assistant keeper at Point Reyes. He went on to become a professional photographer and also to write Beacons of Light. Photograph courtesy of the Jaehne family

(From left) Carl, Herm, Alice, and Claude Jaehne at Point Reyes about 1930
The four happy, mischievous Jaehne kids kept things lively at Point Reyes. "Our mother was sweet," says Alice. "She was so easy. Nothing bothered Mother," adds Herman. Photograph courtesy of the Jaehne family

Alice picks up, "I remember Christmas at Point Reyes. We didn't have lights on the tree, but we'd decorate the tree real nice and put candles on. We could just leave them on for a few minutes because of the danger, but we kids would get so excited at the sight!

"One Christmas there was a BIG box under the tree for me. I couldn't wait to open it! I unwrapped the box, and there was just another box. So I unwrapped it too–nothing but another box. By the time I got to the third box, I was crying and everyone else was laughing. I kept unwrapping boxes and finally got down to a small box that held a play manicure set with a nail file, scissors, and several other things. I still have it today.

"Dad was always pulling tricks on us. One day we got home from school and Dad was holding what looked like a whole apple. He pulled on the top, and the whole thing unraveled like a big spiral! We were fascinated–and he convinced us he had done it himself. Some time later we found out he had purchased an apple peeler! He loved a joke."

A favorite memory of Herman's was Keeper Jaehne buying a candy bar when he went into town. Herman would go to visit his father while he was on watch, and without asking, Herman received a big piece of the prize. Carl and Claude, the two older brothers, would go in to their father and demand a piece. "Dad gave them tiny little pieces. Then I'd go back in and he'd hand me another big piece," Herman says with a smile exactly like the one he must have worn as a kid sixty-five years earlier.

"Our parents were so caring," Alice points out. "Even in the 1920s we were told to never get into a stranger's car. One day we were tired and a big, fancy car pulled up and asked if we knew the way to Point Reyes. We told them we lived there. Did we want a ride home? Oh, no, none of us would get into that car! When we got home, Dad and the visitors were at the lighthouse. 'Those your children, Keeper Jaehne? You sure taught them well–they wouldn't get into our car,' " Alice recalls.

The Jaehnes had a 1911 Hudson. "I don't remember where we parked that car," says Alice, "but I do remember the first time we visited the big city. There we were, looking up with disbelief at all those tall buildings. Hicks from the sticks," she laughs.

In 1931 Keeper Jaehne accepted a transfer, and the family moved into the spacious double keepers' house at Pigeon Point Light Station, only 3 miles away from a town that had an elementary and a high school with thirty-five students. The Jaehne children would come to love this new home–for the remainder of their childhood years and beyond. At Pigeon Point they had fresh vegetables and raised chickens in their yard, and the beach had warmer, calmer water and sand. "We loved to take our boat out to ride the swells," Alice comments. "All our friends from the Gasos Creek school and later the high school at Pescadero loved to visit us."

Herman goes on, "I once took a man out to catch fish for the aquarium in San Francisco. One of my brothers built a pole with a heavy, blunt wire hook, and we hooked an eight-foot octopus. He must have weighed eighty or ninety pounds, and we put him in a big tub the man pumped oxygen into. It became a big attraction at the aquarium.

"Abalone was still plentiful then. We used to gather them in sacks and take them to friends in Pescadero. And fish–so many! We'd gather them for fertilizer for Dad's plants and flowers."

Claude was in daredevil heaven. "He'd climb up on the railing outside the lantern room and walk along it. He'd call down to Mother who was hanging out the clothes, 'LOOK MOM! NO HANDS!' Herman animates.

"One time," Alice recalls with renewed fear, "the boys talked me into climbing from the lower railing up the ladder to the upper railing. I was scared to death. They had to drag me down, stiff-legged, feet first."

Not all was fun and games for the Jaehne children. "We couldn't just come home from school and do homework," Herman says. "We'd get home and Dad would just

The double keepers' house at Pigeon Point Light Station
In 1931 the Jaehne family moved into the spacious double keepers' house at Pigeon Point, just 3 miles away from a town with good-size schools and a beach with warmer, calmer water and sand. It was the happiest place they lived, according to Alice and Herman. Photograph courtesy of the Jaehne family

point his finger up in the air. It meant to get up to the top of the lighthouse and clean the lens inside and the windows outside."

The Jaehne kids savored summer vacations, which afforded more time for fishing, boating, exploring, beachcombing, and freedom to do what they wanted—including summer jobs. Alice worked on farms that raised brussels sprouts and heather—she loved potting plants. The boys worked on vegetable farms. Alice remembers, "Herman would come home with gunny sacks full of peas. We'd all sit around and shell peas."

Herman continues, "We would go into the woods, find wood rats' homes, and sell them to nurseries. One wood rat's home was a pickup load. Come to think of it, I never saw a wood rat, but they must have been big! I loved working in the fields, helping with the irrigation system. Twelve hours a day brought three dollars pay in 1935 through '37."

Both Herman and Alice remember when workers were using a torch to burn old paint off the keeper's house and started a fire. "When the fire started," recalls Alice, "everyone was trying to put it out. We had to wait for the firefighters from Redwood City. That was going to take too long, the boys decided. So they rode their bikes as fast as they could to the gate, got off them, and ran to get the Mexicans working in the field. Well the fire engine came tearing through that gate and ran right over the bicycles." Herman just shakes his head, wanting to forget the episode.

Alice remembers graduating from a bicycle to a car—and back again. "Dad picked me up in our car—he was teaching me to drive. We got to the hill and curve just before the lighthouse, and he stepped on the gas—I guess he wanted to see how I'd react. He sent the car into the ditch and up the hill on the other side. I never drove the car with him again! I went back to a bicycle. Those were the days. With a close family, we didn't have much—we had everything."

In 1939 Keeper Jaehne transferred to the coast guard. At the onset of World War II he came under supervision of the navy, and had the light station come under enemy attack, he would have answered to the army. After the war he once again became a civilian employee wearing the white cap of the U.S. Coast Guard and the gold emblem of the U.S. Lighthouse Service. When sixty-eight-year-old Keeper Jaehne retired in 1952, he received the Gallatin Award, the highest award that can be given to a federal civilian employee.

All four Jaehne children served during the war—Herman as a U.S. Navy aviation radioman, Carl on a U.S. Coast Guard cutter submarine chaser, Alice as a registered nurse in a government hospital, and Claude as a U.S. Navy radioman at Pearl Harbor. "When Claude returned after the attack, he didn't even have any socks," says Herman, shaking his head. Turning serious he adds, "When Claude was thirty-five he went fishing with a friend in Tomales Bay and the boat turned over and Claude drowned." So close to his first lighthouse home at Point Reyes.

Suddenly Herman shouts, "Claude!" But this time it's Claudine, his wife, he's calling to. She's in the kitchen making Dungeness crab sandwiches. Some of Keeper Jaehne's paintings hang over the fireplace in their home, the others having been sold in San Francisco galleries. Alice rocks in a chair next to her brother. Leafing through the family photo album and recalling the memories, a keeper's family is reunited.

FAMILY RECIPES

The first gift Carl gave his mother after he joined the coast guard was a mixer–she loved it and used it often to make noodles, says Alice Jaehne Tierney. Mrs. Jaehne mixed up the dough, rolled it out, and laid the sheets of dough over towels hung on a clothesline stretched across the kitchen. The next day she cut the dried dough into "noodles" and cooked them. Alice and Herman remember eating fresh chicken and noodles for Thanksgiving and Christmas dinners. They also remember their mother's divinity, which she made especially at Christmastime.

DIVINITY

2 cups sugar
1/2 cup light corn syrup
1/4 teaspoon salt

1/2 cup hot water
2 egg whites, stiffly beaten
1 teaspoon vanilla extract

Dissolve the sugar, syrup, and salt in the hot water. Cook without stirring to 248° (firm-ball stage); while the mixture cooks, use a damp cloth to wash down any crystals that form on the sides of the pan. Remove the pan from the heat and gradually pour the syrup mixture over the beaten egg whites, beating constantly with a wire whisk. Add the vanilla and continue beating until the mixture holds its shape when dropped from a spoon. Drop mixture by teaspoonfuls onto waxed paper or spread it into a buttered pan, and score it to be cut into squares later.

Mrs. Jaehne also made a delicious chowder using canned clams and canned milk, the only milk the family had at the light stations.

CLAM CHOWDER

1/4 pound bacon
2 small onions, minced
6 to 8 medium potatoes,
  diced
5 cups cold water

4 cups canned clams
  with their liquid
Salt and pepper
3 cups canned milk

Brown bacon in a deep kettle. Add the minced onions and cook for 2 or 3 minutes. Add the diced potatoes; cover with cold water, heat to boiling, and simmer until the potatoes are tender. Chop the clams; add the chopped clams and their liquid, salt, pepper, and canned milk to the chowder. Heat thoroughly.

POINT REYES LIGHT STATION,

in Point Reyes National Seashore off California Highway 1, is open to the public and attracts about 300,000 visitors annually. Visitors may walk down to the lighthouse except during times of high winds. Bear Valley Visitor Center at the park headquarters houses a gift/bookstore and a museum that features historic documents and lighthouse artifacts. For more information call the Point Reyes Lighthouse Visitors Center at 415/669-1534. The lighthouse is generally open Friday–Monday 10 a.m.–4:30 p.m.

PIGEON POINT LIGHT STATION

is off California Highway 1 about 50 miles south of San Francisco, 25 miles south of Half Moon Bay, and 25 miles north of Santa Cruz. It is now open to the public as a hostel. Office hours begin at 4:30 p.m., and phone reservations are accepted between 7:30 and 9:30 a.m. and 5:30 and 9:30 p.m.

Alice Jaehne in her nurse's uniform during World War II

All four Jaehne children enlisted during World War II. Carl served on a U.S. Coast Guard cutter submarine chaser, Claude served–and survived–as a U.S. Navy radioman at Pearl Harbor, Herman served as a U.S. Navy aviation radioman; and Alice served as a registered nurse at a government hospital. Photograph courtesy of the Jaehne family

The grounds are open year-round. On clear-weather Saturdays and Sundays, tours of the grounds are available. There is a small fee for the guided tours; visitors may also take self-guided tours by purchasing an inexpensive brochure about the light station. For more information contact the California Department of Parks and Recreation, Año Nuevo State Reserve, New Years Creek Road, Pescadero, CA 94060; 650/879-2120.

Photograph by Mark Riddick, New Light Photography

MORRIS ISLAND

ED RESCUES HIS BROTHERS

When the Roaring Twenties were getting started, Edward Vance Hewett was getting started on his keeper's career at Bald Head Light at the mouth of the Cape Fear River in southeastern North Carolina. A year later, when the flappers were dancing the Charleston in Charleston, South Carolina, Keeper Hewett and his family were settling into the assistant keeper's quarters at Morris Island/Charleston Light Station. It was only 15 miles away from the jazzy lights and music, but Morris Island was a whole other world. And just a year later, the Hewetts moved again—this time to historic St. Augustine Light Station in Florida.

Keeper Hewett and his wife, Amanda "Anna" Gore Hewett, raised five lighthouse children—Ed, Benny, Leon, Ruby, and Dottie. Young Ed was eight years old when his father served at the impressive Morris Island Light Station. He shares his memories of some of the adventures he and his brothers survived while living on the island.

In 1920 the U.S. Lighthouse Service hummed along under the steady hand of Commissioner George Putnam. The country struggled to adjust to peacetime after World War I, and inflation reared its ugly head. Cash flow and credit had been increased to help ease the time of transition, but the inevitable increase in cost of living kept spiraling upward.

Americans were learning a hard lesson about postwar recovery. Many had gone for long periods without "frills" such as gasoline for travel, sugar for baking desserts, or enough money for new appliances. Deceitful profiteers had bought up most of these frills, and their seeming rarity sent prices sky-high. The U.S. Lighthouse Service warned its employees to continue a conservative lifestyle—to keep making do. Post–World War I children grew up with an appreciation of possessions and a strong desire to live an independent, productive life.

The U.S. Lighthouse Service overcame a suppressive time, when keepers and administrative positions were political appointees through the president of the United States, and developed into an organization true to the American dream of opportunity in upward mobility. Many of the lighthouse administrators started their careers as sailors or merchant mariners and rose in the ranks with experience. Lighthouse keepers

Morris Island Light Station, better known as Charleston Light, in 1893

During the Civil War the first Charleston Lighthouse met with the same fate as many other southern lights—Confederate soldiers destroyed it to prevent Union forces from controlling shipping lanes. Rebuilt after the war, the tall lighthouse tower protected Charleston's busy harbor. The keepers' dwelling, built in 1874, reflected the then-popular stick-style architecture that had been used for the double keepers' home at Currituck Beach Light Station in Corolla, North Carolina. An extreme storm overwash in the 1930s prompted the lighthouse service to automate Morris Island Lighthouse, eliminating the need for a keeper and ending family life at the station. In 1962 the light was relocated to Sullivans Island, and today the 1874 tower stands alone, dark and surrounded by water. No one will ever again witness the grandeur of this magnificent historic lighthouse. Photograph taken in 1893 by U.S. Light-House Board Engineer Herbert Bamber and reprinted from the James Claflin Collection began at smaller, more remote light stations and worked their way up to more important lights with assistants under their supervision.

Keeper Edward Vance Hewett began his fast-track career in 1920 at Bald Head Light at the mouth of the Cape Fear River in southeastern North Carolina. His first promotion came after only one year's service when he was appointed to the impressive Morris Island Light Station, also known as Charleston Light. He was on his way.

The big three-story frame house at Morris Island accommodated Head Keeper Hewett and his family as well as the two assistant keepers' families. "My family lived upstairs, and my room was on the northwest corner," Ed says about the grand home that once complemented the lighthouse tower.

In 1921 Ed, Benny, Leon, and Ruby were the only children at the light station—or on the island, for that matter (Dottie was born in 1925 at St. Augustine). Ed's father bought him a 10-foot rowboat with a sail and taught him how to maneuver it. Ed says, "We

Keeper Vance Hewett, Anna Hewett, and Ruby

Ed comments, "This picture of my dad and mother and my sister Ruby was taken in 1924 on the ruins of the old Spanish lighthouse. Waves and erosion put the old lighthouse into the sea in Salt Run at St. Augustine on August 22, 1880, and the site is now under water."

Photograph courtesy of Ed Hewett Shepherd

had a long dock across the marshy area behind the lighthouse. We kept our boat docked there and had at least a quarter mile between us and the ocean. We used to play on the river. I was only eight years old when I learned to sail a ten-foot boat!"

Eight-year-old Ed was big brother to seven-year-old Leon and five-year-old Bennie. One day Ed offered to take his brothers to Folly Island in the boat, giving them a chance to play out *Treasure Island.* The tide was low and the wind blew right and the three boys crossed the river to Folly Island without a care in the world. Ed and his brothers pulled the boat way up on the sandy beach to prevent the high tide from stealing it, and then, as an added safety measure, they dragged the anchor even higher up on the

Morris Island Light Station in 1923

"We took this picture from the walkway leading to the dock at Morris Island Light Station when we were leaving for St. Augustine Light Station in 1923 on the buoy tender U.S.S. Waterlily," says Ed, the eldest son of Keeper Vance Hewett. "The fence around the light station was brick, and the gate was iron." In the years since then, Morris Island has all but disappeared, and today the lighthouse stands alone with water lapping at the base. Wind and water have erased all traces of the keepers' dwelling and the families who lived in it. Photograph courtesy of Ed Hewett Shepherd

shore. Confidently the three Robinson Crusoes took off down the beach keeping their eye out for anything out of the ordinary. Only two years before, in the closing months of World War I, Ed had seen a German submarine pop up close to Bald Head Island, and he often found parts of old wooden sailing ships and even a pirate's rusted flintlock pistol in the treasure-rich sand.

A recent storm had plowed out a lake a few hundred feet inland from the beach, and when the boys discovered it, they decided to take a swim to cool off after their hot boat ride. Leon and Bennie found a palmetto log and floated it out toward the center of the lake, pretending they were Crusoe and Man Friday, while Ed waded close to shore hunting for treasures. Ed looked up after a few minutes and didn't see any sign of his little brothers—he just saw bubbles coming up near the palmetto log. Scared to death he swam out to the log, held onto it, and kicked his way to the bubbles. With one arm clamped around the log, he reached down, grabbed a handful of hair, and nearly snatching Leon bald-headed, pulled him up while kicking the log to shore.

"All I could think of was to get the water out of Leon," said Ed. "I held him up by his feet and hit him in the back. He coughed and started breathing. I knew I had to work fast. Shaking like a weak pup, I put Leon down, took hold of the log, and headed back to the middle of the lake where I had seen more bubbles."

Ed called upon every ounce of his remaining energy fueled by adrenaline. He reached down through the bubbles, grabbed Bennie's hair, pulled him up, and struggled to get to shore. "Again, the only thing I knew to do was try and get the water out of him," Ed said excitedly. "I held him up by the legs and shook him and then hit him in the back—and it worked! I sure did shake some water out of Bennie before he got his breath. He was in pretty bad shape, but he finally did start spitting water and crying. I was so worried about Bennie.

"I tried to calm him, and after a while he quieted down. Leon was almost recovered by then and helped me get Bennie back to the boat. The tide was already getting high, but I put up the sail and rowed as hard as I could, and we got back across the river to the dock at the lighthouse. Bennie could have died. But I just beat the water out of him!" Ed chuckles, but not without due respect for what might have happened.

"I hated to tell Mama about what had happened," Ed continues. "Leon was okay, but Bennie was going to need at least a few days to dry out. I started my explanation several times before I could get the whole story out. And Mama took it calmly," Ed states. "She told me I was a good son and smart and had done the right thing. But Leon and Bennie never again would go to that island with me!"

Ed always loved to explore—it just seemed the natural thing to do with all the wonderful places and new creatures to experience. He often could be seen going down the long walkway from the house to the dock. On the west side of the dock was the boathouse for the lighthouse boat Keeper Hewett used to go to Charleston for mail and supplies. On the east side was the mouth of the river that connected Morris Island to Folly Island, and it was here that Ed kept his own rowboat, the "frigate" he captained and took out on some very important jobs.

One day Ed headed down the dock for another reason. He had been eyeing a big area of oysters near the dock for a long time and waiting for some time alone when he could figure out how to get those delicious shellfish out of the water and onto the Hewett family's dinner table. The young explorer overestimated his skill of balance that day, though, and as he reached over the dock with his specially designed oyster retriever, Ed says, "I ended up in bed with the oysters.

Keeper Vance Hewett with Leon and Bennie at St. Augustine Lighthouse in 1924

Keeper Vance Hewett, dressed in full uniform, took his two youngest sons, Leon and Bennie, to the top of St. Augustine Lighthouse for this picture. Young Bennie looks as if he is braced against a stiff wind and contemplating the height. Photograph courtesy of Ed Hewett Shepherd

"When I walked out of that bed of oysters, I was cut all over from the top of my head to the bottom of my feet," says Ed, still with some disbelief. "I got back on the dock and ran the whole way to the house. My mama and the first keeper's wife were standing by the gate talking."

Ed vaguely remembers his mother looking as pale as a ghost at the sight of her bludgeoned son. He doesn't remember any more because "for the first and only time in my life, I passed out!" Ed laughs aloud. When he came to he was wrapped in bandages made out of sheets and he reeked of the turpentine someone had poured into the thousand slits in his body.

The saltwater and sun healed his cuts quickly, and three days later Ed was back on the beach looking for flounder and using a pitchfork to spear ones that were trapped in pools of water left at high tide. Evidently the memory of that serious scrape is still vivid, and Ed says he was always more cautious whenever

Ed (age twelve), Bennie (age eight), and Leon (age ten) at St. Augustine Light Station in 1925
Big brother Ed takes a protective pose with the two brothers he saved from drowning.
Photograph courtesy of Ed Hewett Shepherd

he leaned over the edge of a dock after that day more than six decades ago.

Not long after that incident Keeper Hewett applied for a transfer to a light station where his children could go to school. The lighthouse service understood the needs of the keepers' families and made Ed's father the first assistant keeper at St. Augustine Lighthouse in Florida. Although the light station is on Anastasia Island, a trolley line ran over the bridge to the mainland, and the school was only about a mile from the trolley stop. Like most lighthouse children, Ed and his siblings traveled quite a distance through all kinds of weather to gain an education.

And school was where Ed caught different things that next year, things he hadn't caught while living in relative isolation on Morris Island–mumps, measles, chicken pox, and whooping cough. And being a sharing brother, Ed also gave them to Leon and Bennie. The boys had never been sick a day on Morris Island.

"And they made me start in the first grade!" Ed still wails in disgust. "I felt so funny and out of place being almost ten and in the first grade–three years older than the other kids."

But Ed adjusted and became educated and has lived a full life, proud of his lighthouse family heritage. "Dad, Mama, all of us worked awfully hard those years Dad was in the service. We helped each other, and the light [beacon] always came first. Those were the good ol' days."

FAMILY RECIPE

Ed says this is Anna Hewett's favorite cookie recipe. She gave it to Ed's wife when they married fifty-five years ago. He also says that these cookies are SO GOOD–the best of all cookies!

NUT CRUNCHIES

1½ cups sifted all-purpose flour
½ teaspoon baking soda
½ teaspoon salt
½ cup shortening or 1 stick margarine
½ cup brown sugar
½ cup white sugar
1 egg, well-beaten
1 teaspoon vanilla
1 cup broken pecans
½ cup raisins

Sift together flour, baking soda, and salt. Cream together shortening, brown sugar, and white sugar. Add egg to creamed mixture and mix well. Add vanilla, pecans, and raisins to creamed mixture and mix well. Gradually add flour mixture to creamed mixture.

Drop dough by teaspoonfuls onto cookie sheets. Bake at 300°-325° for about 10 minutes or until lightly browned.

MORRIS ISLAND LIGHTHOUSE, just off the coast of South Carolina near Charleston, is best viewed at Folly Beach. A local group is trying to save the lighthouse, which stands nearly 100 yards off Folly Beach and is frequently surrounded by water. For more information contact Save the Light committee at 843/633-0099.

Saddleback Ledge Light Station,
Maine

SADDLEBACK LEDGE TENANTS HARBOR

KEEPER AND DAUGHTER LIGHT THE LAMP

Leonard Bosworth Dudley accepted his first U.S. Lighthouse Service assignment in 1909, when daughter June was a year old. During his thirty-one-year career, Keeper Dudley served at West Quoddy Head (near Lubec), Saddleback Ledge (off Vinalhaven Island), and Tenants Harbor (on Southern Island), all in Maine–the lighthouse state. Unfortunately many of Maine's lighthouses now lie in disrepair, left in the wake of navigational technology. Orphaned by the coast guard, a number of them have been adopted by individuals and groups and are being restored with the help of state and federal aid.

June was her father's constant companion and helper, and she provides one of the few living links with Maine's rich lighthouse history. In her sparse New England style, June shares her fondest memories of working alongside her dad to keep the lights burning.

M y father began as a substitute keeper at West Quoddy Head Light Station, outside Lubec, Maine. Subs weren't easy to find in those days–at least subs the lighthouse service could depend on," June begins. Dad was excited to begin his career. He had been on ships before and wanted to stay close to the water. Plus, he loved Maine–he never would have left Maine."

Mariners who were fishing or traversing the frigid North Atlantic waters depended on Maine's lights–famous Portland Head Light, the stately Two Lights at Cape Elizabeth, formidable Matinicus Rock and Saddleback Ledge Lights, quaint Brown's Head Light, dramatic Pemaquid Point Light, powerful Seguin Island Light, stubby Owl's Head Light, and peaceful Rockland Breakwater Light, which is tethered to the shore by a rocky leash. Raging sou'westers left over from tropical origins, freezing storms out of Canada, and sudden, desultory storms wreaked havoc on large and small ships alike. "Several times when my father was at Tenants Harbor, or we called it Southern Island, he had to take the boat across to town to call the coast guard and have them come get boats that got stranded off the island. Once Dad went out with them during a storm and

West Quoddy Head Light Station, near Lubec, Maine, in 1990

West Quoddy Head Light Station stands on the northeasternmost tip of the continental United States and faces East Quoddy Head Light Station on Canada's Campobello Island. Leonard Dudley began his U.S. Lighthouse Service career in 1909, when daughter June was a year old. "My father served as a substitute keeper at West Quoddy Head Light. Subs weren't easy to find in those days—at least subs the lighthouse service could depend on," says June.

helped pull a boat off the bar with a rope," recalls June.

"It could always be tricky when the fishermen came in the 'back shore way.' Dad always tried to help, even if it was dangerous. Sometimes my mother, sister, and I tried to watch, but most of the time I found myself with my eyes squeezed shut tight. I just couldn't stand to see something happen to my father."

June was learning responsibilities as any teenager would when Keeper Dudley served at Saddleback Ledge Light Station, which clings to a chunk of granite that pops up out of the Atlantic at the entrance to East Penobscot Bay. According to U.S. Lighthouse Service records, Saddleback Ledge was completed in 1839 following the tragic burning of the

Royal Tar, which was carrying circus performers and their animals in 1836. Ice covers the rock in winter months, and sometimes keepers could not leave the station for weeks or occasionally months at a time. Gales washed over the island, and landing at the site was so difficult that in 1885 a landing derrick was built for getting on and off the island. June came to know the island–and the derrick–well.

"I'll never forget being picked up by the derrick and swinging in the bosun's chair. If it was rough and the men couldn't bring the boat in, the assistant would lower the seat down, WAY down into the water. I'd climb in, and up we'd go." June remembers how good it felt to fall into the soft warmth of her father's strong arms after her heart-pumping ride. "He was a big, handsome man," June says.

"There were three keepers stationed at Saddleback Ledge. One of the keepers would go home for eight days while the other two stayed on the island full-time. I missed Dad so much that sometimes I was allowed to go and stay with him for maybe two days at a time. Assistant Ed Howell is the man I remember most. He would take an old oilcan and throw it into the water and we would play a game with my father to see who could hit

Matinicus Rock Lighthouse in 1995
Like Abbie Burgess Grant, a New England heroine, June served as her father's unofficial assistant keeper. Abbie lived on Matinicus Rock during the 1850s and '60s, a half-century before June and her father kept the light burning at Saddleback Ledge. Photograph by Cheryl Shelton-Roberts

Saddleback Ledge Light Station about 1921

June used a kitchen knife to remove this picture from the tattered pages of an old album. She often visited her father while he was on duty on Saddleback Ledge Light Station, off Vinalhaven Island in Maine. To hear the happiness in June's voice as she recalls being at Saddleback Ledge with her father, you might think they were at some plush resort instead of a sterile outcropping of rock. "He was so handsome, and he was such a good father," June comments with respect. "He taught me to depend upon myself and that I could do anything. I was his shadow, doing whatever he did. I often went up the stairs for him and lit the lamp," she adds. "I guess he was afraid of heights." Photograph courtesy of June Dudley Watts

it with a rock. He'd always grin at me and ask, 'Miss June, you want to put one of those cans overboard?' I loved to play that game. We'd throw rocks and see who was best.

"I remember once when something happened that was the most frightening thing I've ever known." With renewed fear in her eyes, June goes on, "I was at the water's edge with Dad and Mr. Howell, who was chipping rocks off with a hammer for me to throw. All of a sudden he said, 'Cappie,' that's what he called my dad because he was head, I think we'd better go and get in out of this—there's a tidal wave coming.' WAY off in the distance we saw the water forming a wall and coming up and up, bigger and bigger.

" 'Well my sakes,' my father said, 'we'd better get the shutters over the windows because that definitely looks like a tidal wave. Maybe two.'

"I think in about two hours, the water came right in over that house at Saddleback, down the chimney. I was so frightened, honest. Dad said, 'Now, June, there's nothing we can do.' My heart was pounding, and I thought, 'Dad will make it all right.' And he said, 'We just have to wait 'til this is over.' I think there were three of those HUGE waves," June says raising her arms and making big circles.

"I don't know what ever made those waves. I looked in the kitchen and the stovepipe had fallen from the flue and the water was pouring into the floor as big as that," she says holding her arms and hands in as big a circle as her small frame allows. "I can still see my father now–he was down on the floor with a pail and the brass dustpan, scooping up the water. And I bet it was two feet deep on the floor. He wasn't doing much good, but he had to do something! The waves passed. But my heart would never calm down.

"The light was all right. It's a wonder it didn't wash the shingles away. The men had to check everything. It was terrifying," June concludes. "We worried while Dad was out there alone so much of the time with just one other man to help, but after this, I really worried."

That wasn't the first time waves had inundated the tower and house at Saddleback Ledge. There is a story about a fifteen-year-old boy who was on the island with his father, the keeper, and provisions were getting low. The father rowed to the mainland to get supplies and ended up being held hostage onshore for three weeks by stormy seas,

leaving his young son on the island alone to keep the fourth-order lens lit. When the father finally made it back to the island, he found his son safe but weak.

June readily relates to another keeper's daughter, Abbie Burgess Grant, who lived at Matinicus Rock Light Station in the 1850s. Twice fourteen-year-old Abbie was stranded for several weeks at Matinicus, more than 20 miles offshore. In addition to taking care of her invalid mother and younger sisters, Abbie kept the fourteen lamps lit in each of the two towers on the

Principal Keeper Dudley (at the top of the stairs) with his two assistant keepers and a visiting worker at Saddleback Ledge Light Station about 1921
"Sometimes work crews came to do heavier repairs on the lighthouse," June remembers.
Photograph courtesy of June Dudley Watts

June riding in a bosun's chair at Saddleback Ledge Light Station about 1920
"I'll never forget being picked up by the derrick and swinging in the bosun's chair," June smiles. When weather made a landing too risky, which was more often than not, an assistant would lower the bosun's chair, June would climb in, and she would be hauled up for a safe landing on—or a safe departure from—the rough rock of the island. Photograph courtesy of June Dudley Watts

island. One time storm waves washed away part of the keeper's house only a short time after Abbie had moved her sisters and mother to safety in one of the towers. As if twice weren't enough, Abbie was stranded two more times at Matinicus, then married to Isaac Grant, when her father-in-law, John Grant, served as the keeper.

June says, "Wherever my dad went, I was right behind. I was afraid when the waves washed over the house and during many storms while we lived together, but I knew we would survive. But I sure did worry about him a lot when he was on the island. It was such a happy time when he came home."

June did her share of work when she stayed at the light station with her father. "My goodness, I guess I did polish some brass–and everything else that ever had to be cleaned by a keeper. Dad was always busy repairing something or making something or cleaning something. I had to paint, wash floors, everything."

One of June's happiest memories of her lighthouse childhood is when Keeper Dudley transferred to the light station on Southern Island about half a mile offshore from Tenants Harbor on the mainland. "Being a keeper was very hard–not everybody could do what my father did," says June. "Oh, yes, I helped! I helped milk our Bossy cow, take care of hens–oh, my I guess I was my father's assistant.

"Sometimes a keeper needed a rescue too," June's diction becomes almost childish as she reveals a lifelong secret. "I had to go up the tower every afternoon and go outside by the railing and clean the windows. Heights, outside the tower especially, bothered my dad–I guess he was afraid of heights," June grins.

June says the hardest work was cleaning the windows, sometimes in razor-edged winds and sea spray. "But I would do those windows for him. He couldn't climb the ladder and work on the roof or the tower–the assistants did that.

Principal Keeper Leonard Dudley (center) and two assistant keepers with their U.S. Lighthouse Service-issued launch at Saddleback Ledge Light Station about 1921

June Dudley Watts treasures pictures of her father. Although Keeper Dudley and the others appear relaxed, June states, "They were waiting for the inspector to arrive." Photograph courtesy of June Dudley Watts

"I cleaned the windows on the inside too sometimes. I would use something Dad gave me in a can. It was always a big job to make sure clean, soft rags were kept all the time. We didn't have paper towels then, don't you know. I climbed that tower on Southern Island often. I'll never forget this–those are my happiest memories. Yes, I worked hard, but I was so independent then. Almost like a boy."

June continues, "I trimmed the wick many times too. Dad taught me how and kept me in practice just in case. I would use a five-gallon oilcan and fill the bottom of the lamp and trim the wick–it always reminded me of Aladdin's lamp with a mantle and one round wick. The lamp had a red chimney and some panels that turned by clock-work so the light flashed red. Dad used a match to light the wick.

"I remember some of the storms we had–they were almost like hurricanes many times. The surf would come in, way up, great big rolls almost to the fog-bell tower. It was scary. And Dad couldn't leave his post, and we weren't going to leave him. We had no communication with the mainland, no telephone. And we used kerosene lamps. But we didn't miss a thing.

"My sister, Hazel, and I loved the beach at Southern Island. But we didn't play much. I went down, sometimes alone, to gather wood for burning in our cookstove. I worked,

but I consider myself almost spoiled then. I tell you, I loved to wear knickerbockers and a hat. The greatest times were when the family all gathered together for reunions. So much food and lots of cousins to play with. My father was very proud of what he did.

"Dad rowed me to school at Tenants Harbor every day about seven in the morning. Later we used the powerboat lighthouse service provided. And I loved to go across in the boat alone to get groceries. Yes, I was allowed to go alone–I would find any excuse possible to get to go across. I liked to knit and crochet, and there was a shop

June at Tenants Harbor Light Station about 1923
June admits, "I was always independent. I liked to dress like a boy." Here she's wearing fancy knickers and a beret. "Living at Tenants Harbor was the happiest time of my life," June says. Photograph courtesy of June Dudley Watts

that I would go to and get whatever I wanted or needed. One day on a trip for lots of things, when I was nineteen years old, I met Everett Watts. He was a lobster fisherman and very shy like me. Everett offered to help me carry all my packages to my boat. I said, 'No.'

"The next time I came in, Everett offered to help tie off my boat. I didn't say anything. Well, the next day, he comes to Southern Island. He had been very nice all those times trying to help me, and I told Dad so. Dad was working in his garden and didn't look very happy at first to see Everett. But since we had visitors so little, he decided he liked Everett after all. Everett asked me to marry him.

"We had the minister all engaged up the road from Tenants Harbor. Of course Everett and I were all dressed up and ready to go. We walked up to the minister's front door and knocked. We told him we were ready for him to marry us. He said, 'Well, I am very, very sorry, but I just had a whole house full of company come in, so we'll have to postpone it.'

"I said, 'Listen, dear reverend, to postpone it means bad luck. No, we're not going to postpone it.' Everett and I thought that he didn't need our business, so we left and went to a friend of Everett's at Rockport and asked him if would do the job. 'Willingly,' he answered. So we were married up at Rockport. For our honeymoon we went to Boston on the steamer *City of Boston*. A man Everett knew invited us to the Copely Plaza Hotel in Boston as his guests," June says proudly. "So we stayed there three days and did the city of Boston. He wouldn't take a penny—it was a wedding gift."

June leafs through a family photo album. She becomes discouraged as she points to several pictures and comments, "He's gone and he's gone and she's gone—they're all gone now.

"Aha!" June brightens again. "There are my dad and mumma and Hazel and June—that's me—at Tenants Harbor on Southern Island. Those were always happy times together."

FAMILY RECIPE

Keeper Leonard Dudley loved lobster stew. June remembers her mother making this recipe often, a dish fit for a king, and to June, her father was a king. June says her mother added fresh ingredients from her father's garden like bell peppers, tomatoes, parsley, and scallions.

LOBSTER STEW

Cooking the lobsters:
3 or 4 "chicken" lobsters
3 quarts salted water (The Dudleys used some of the seawater the lobsters were kept in until they were cooked.)

Bring the salted water to boiling, and boil the lobsters until they turn bright red (about 20 minutes). Let lobsters cool; remove all the meat (you should have about 3½ cups of meat).

Basic stew:
6 white or red potatoes
2½ quarts water
Butter
¾ to 1 cup finely diced or grated carrot
¾ to 1 cup finely diced or grated onion
¾ cup thinly chopped celery
3 to 4 cups milk (The Dudleys usually used government-issued canned milk and diluted it.)
Salt and pepper to taste

Cut potatoes into quarters and boil in 2½ quarts water for about 20 minutes or until fork-tender; keep potatoes and broth warm (do not drain potatoes). Melt butter and saute other vegetables for about 5 minutes. Add the sauteed vegetables, milk, lobster meat, salt, and pepper to the potatoes and broth; let stew simmer slowly for at least an hour.
Serve with fresh cornbread.

SADDLEBACK LEDGE LIGHT STATION stands alone on a remote rock about 6 miles east of Vinalhaven Island off the coast of Maine. Landing on the island is extremely dangerous, but the lighthouse can be viewed from a private cruise boat or airplane.

TENANTS HARBOR LIGHT STATION, located on Southern Island, is privately owned by the Wyeth family and is closed to the public. It can be viewed from the town of Tenants Harbor, Maine, located about one and one-half hours drive north of Portland Head on Maine Highway 131. Just a bit farther north is Rockland, Maine, the home of the Rockland Breakwater Lighthouse and the outstanding Shore Village Museum, which houses one of the largest collections of Fresnel lenses in America.

WEST QUODDY HEAD LIGHT STATION is in Quoddy Head State Park, outside Lubec, Maine. From U.S. 1 take Maine Highway 189 toward Lubec, turn right into the state park, and continue about 5 miles to the lighthouse parking area. Visitors may tour the grounds and keeper's quarters, also called the Visitor Center, which is open generally from Memorial Day through Columbus Day weekend. The lighthouse is still owned and maintained by the U.S. Coast Guard and is open twice a year: the Saturday after the Fourth of July and one day in September. For more information, call the West Quoddy Head Visitor Center at 207/733-2180.

PONCE DE LEON INLET

THE LIGHTHOUSE CHILD

Edward Lockwood Meyer served in the U.S. Merchant Marine during World War I and joined the U.S. Lighthouse Service in 1923. During his twenty-two-year career he served as keeper at St. Augustine (1923-26), Ponce de Leon (1926-30 and 1937-43), and Jupiter Inlet (1930-33)—all in Florida, Morris Island (1933-35) and Charleston Harbor lights (1935-37) in South Carolina, and Sombrero Key Reef (1943) and Loggerhead Key (1944-45) in Florida. Edward and Ellen Mary Sheehan Meyer had six children, four of them born at light stations—Jack and Betty at the assistant keeper's house at St. Augustine, Mary at Jupiter Inlet, and Gladys at the assistant keeper's house at Ponce de Leon Inlet Light Station on the Fourth of July 1928. Today Gladys lives in her family's house just down the street from where she was born. She shares her memories of living at and working to preserve light stations.

Gladys says, "My father was in the U.S. Merchant Marine service during World War I. His brother, William, lived in New York City at that time. Upon returning to the States at a port in New York, my father went to visit his brother and his wife, Sophie Bennett. It just so happened that Sophie's best friend, Ellen Mary Sheehan, was visiting at the same time. Over dinner Edward and Ellen Mary discovered they had a great deal in common, and the rest is history. They were married in Charleston, near my father's birthplace on St. John's Island, South Carolina, on August 20, 1919. My parents were on their way to enjoying a long and adventurous life together.

"There were two children born while they lived in Charleston. My sister Gertrude died at nine months of age from a kidney ailment during the time before antibiotics. My mother spoke of the baby up until the day she passed away. She learned that children are not possessions and that tomorrow is not to be counted upon. Doing one's best in the present moment is all the chance we have. These values were passed on to us other five kids.

"My father joined the U.S. Lighthouse Service in 1923 and was first stationed at St. Augustine Lighthouse in Florida, where he served as first assistant keeper. My brother Jack was born there on October 6, 1924, and my sister Betty on April 20, 1926. Later

Jupiter Inlet Light Station, Florida

This lighthouse warns mariners away from the treacherous reef at Jupiter Inlet, just north of the Palm Beach area of Florida. "I was just two years old when my family transferred to Jupiter Inlet," Gladys comments. "My younger sister, Mary, was born here in 1932, completing our lighthouse family."

Father was transferred as first assistant keeper to Ponce de Leon Inlet Lighthouse in Florida, where I was born in 1928."

Since medical help was not readily available in remote areas, the U.S. Lighthouse Service provided each keeper's family with a chest containing the basic medical supplies of the day, including iodine, tooth pullers, and morphine, which was only to be administered by the keeper on doctor's orders. In the days before antibiotics, however, lighthouse children—like other children—often suffered deafness from ear infections; died from diarrhea, colds, or diphtheria; or like Gladys suffered from allergies.

At eighteen months Gladys weighed only 18 pounds, refused to eat, and wasn't expected to live to celebrate her second birthday. Her mother persisted, however, until she found a doctor who determined that "acidosis" was causing Gladys's slow growth and food intolerance. Now, after celebrating many decades of birthdays, Gladys proudly says, "I fooled them all!

"Our young family moved to isolated Ponce de Leon Inlet Lighthouse by car," she continues. Here, no transportation was available. As a result, my brother Edward missed his first year of school."

The original 1835 Ponce de Leon tower was never lit–a storm badly damaged the foundation and hostile Seminole Indians wouldn't allow workers to repair it. The replacement tower, built on the north side of the inlet, reached an impressive 175 feet, ranking second only to Cape Hatteras among the tallest lighthouses on the East Coast. Gladys remembers climbing the 203 steps of the spiral staircase to the lantern room–and she remembers the BUGS. "Yes, the area earned well the alias 'Mosquito Inlet.' To

U.S. Lighthouse Service-issued medicine chest on display at Ponce de Leon Light Station museum

The U.S. Lighthouse Service issued medicine chests that included quinine pills, castor oil, sweet spirits of niter, opium, and camphor pills. These medicines were the only readily available medical care for keepers and their families living on islands and other remote outposts where the closest doctor was hours–or even days–away. The opium and other potent medicines were to be administered only by the keeper on the advice of a doctor. Sometimes when a doctor was needed, the keeper would raise a flag and hope that someone on the mainland or a passing boat would get the message and summon help.

When the U.S. Coast Guard took over control of the lighthouses in 1939 and came to "clean out" Ponce de Leon Light Station, Keeper Edward Meyer kept this medicine chest so it wouldn't be declared "surplus" and discarded. "The coastguardsmen from New Smyrna Beach were very helpful during the move," says Gladys, who still lives in the house the family settled in permanently just a few blocks from the light station. The medicine chest Gladys's father rescued is now on display at the museum at Ponce de Leon Light Station.

Morris Island Light Station, South Carolina

Keeper Meyer and his family moved from Jupiter Inlet, Florida, to the double keepers' house at Morris Island, South Carolina, in 1933. Through the ironwork gate in the fence surrounding the light station, Gladys watched her family's belongings and livestock wash away in a storm surge in 1935. "My strongest memories about living on Morris Island are of the storms, Christmas, and my German shepherd, Wolf, who adopted a kitten," says Gladys. Photograph taken in 1893 by U.S. Light-House Board Engineer Herbert Bamber and reprinted from the James Claflin Collection

add insult to injury, the mosquitoes traveled with other pests known as 'no see-ums.' You know, those nasty little black flies that bite–and HURT!

"Next my family transferred to Jupiter Inlet Lighthouse in 1930. My younger sister, Mary, was born here in 1932, completing our lighthouse family."

In 1933 the Meyer family moved to Charleston, where Gladys's father served as keeper at Morris Island Light Station. Gladys recalls her father planting a vegetable garden on the island to help provide healthier food for his family and to ease the inconvenience of no nearby stores.

Today Morris Island is under water, but Gladys still remembers how much "fun" it was to walk along the 500-foot narrow boardwalk from the boathouse to the keeper's dwelling. All five of the young Meyer children could swim, but that didn't seem to soothe their mother's anxiety as she watched them make the precarious trek each time they left or returned to their lighthouse home. "Father often would take the family over the thread of walk connecting our living space to the boat provided by the U.S. Lighthouse Service to cross the river to Folly Island. There we would patiently wait for him to walk the mile to a garage where he proudly started his Model T, then returned to pick us up, and away we'd go to the big city. In Charleston my family would collect the mail, buy needed supplies, and then make the journey home doing the same in reverse.

"One time Father decided to hire two rowboats and two brave men to lash the Model T onto the small vessels and float the car back to the island. It became an object of curiosity as people would fly overhead and wonder how in the world those people got that car on that island. The car was a wonderful distraction in an isolated area, and we and the other family that lived there would take turns riding back and forth on the short strip crossing the barrier island. There were now five children in our family, and there were five children in the other family—and ten kids got a lot of kicks from our wonderful Model T.

"Both families lived in a three-story wooden duplex on Morris Island, similar to the keeper's house at St. Augustine.

The Meyer family Model T being "rowed" to Morris Island

Gladys laughs as she explains, "One time Father decided to hire two rowboats and two brave men to lash the Model T onto the small vessels and float the car back to Morris Island. It became an object of curiosity as people would fly overhead and wonder how in the world those people got that car on that island. It was a wonderful distraction in an isolated area, and we and the other keeper's family took turns riding back and forth on the short strip of road that crossed the island." Photograph courtesy of Gladys Meyer Davis

(From left) Principal Keeper John Linquist, a visitor, and Assistant Keeper Edward Meyer at St. Augustine Lighthouse in 1924

Gladys says, "I'm sure my father was called from a task he was performing to have this picture taken with the visitor—he never would have appeared with grease spots on his pants otherwise. I learned meticulous cleaning from my mother and father. Even now when I start doing housework my husband, Earl, tells me 'Gladys, the inspector is not coming today.'" Photograph courtesy of Gladys Meyer Davis

There was no school available the first year, so my two older brothers and my sister resided during the week with our grandparents on St. John's Island in order to attend school. They would return each Friday evening to rejoin the family.

"What fun it was to take rides on the beach in the Model T. And it was fun to swim and catch all the crabs we could eat on the beach. I remember our pet on the island, a beautiful and lovable German shepherd named Wolf. Someone brought a black kitten to the island, and Wolf adopted her. He would carry the kitten in his mouth, just like a mother cat, all around the yard. I still smile when I think of those two—they were inseparable."

Keeper Meyer's family lived in Charleston, and he hosted family get-togethers on Morris Island. Gladys remembers the entire clan going oyster digging and sitting around the oak kitchen table cracking roasted shellfish.

"With the help of my father's brother-in-law, who was on the board of education in Charleston, a one-room school was established on the lighthouse grounds. There were eight grades in one room. My family furnished the very young teacher with a room, and the other family furnished her board."

In 1935 a tremendous storm surge swept over Morris Island, and Gladys watched as water rushed over the high concrete walls encasing the light station compound and washed away their chickens, pigs, turkeys, and all of their other animals. "In desperation I cried for Father to close the open-ironwork gates!" she remembers. As they continued to watch in horror, they saw the angry floodwaters take one more sacrifice—their precious Model T. A short time later, the Meyer family packed what they could salvage and left Morris Island–they were the last family to live at the light station.

In 1937 Gladys and her family returned to Ponce de Leon Inlet Lighthouse, where her father had accepted the position of principal keeper. Gladys remembers her father helping many people who were injured in shipwrecks on the dangerous reef at the inlet. She also recalls how isolated she and her brothers and sisters felt at Ponce de Leon and some of the mischief her brothers devised to relieve their boredom. "Once my brothers put a note in a bottle and threw it off the lighthouse dock. The note said, 'Stranded on Grass Island.' This was a small island covered with sea grass across the river from the lighthouse dock. The bottle was picked up by a coastguardsman stationed at New Smyrna and brought to the lighthouse. Upon seeing the note my father knew where it had come from but did not let my brothers know right away that he knew they were responsible for it. They were two mighty scared youngsters and just knew they would be in a lot of trouble with the authorities. They admitted they had put the note in the bottle and received a stern lecture. There was no harm done, but they never tried that prank again."

All five Meyer children attended the elementary school in Port Orange, Florida. Although they were near the school, just 6 miles across the river on the mainland, there was no easy way to get there. Every morning at 7:30 they walked a short distance to catch the bus driven by their neighbor Mr. B. G. Timmons, rode 12 miles north on Atlantic Avenue to Orange Avenue Bridge in Daytona Beach (the first bridge to the mainland), and then turned back south 6 miles to the school.

Eventually the Meyer children grew to

Keeper Edward Meyer holding daughter Gladys, with sons Edward and Jack standing in front, on the dock at Ponce de Leon Inlet in 1930

"I was about two years old when my Aunt Marie, my mother's sister, took this picture. She was quite a photographer. We have many photos because she would visit from New York and bring along her newfangled camera and take lots of pictures of her favorite lighthouse family," says Gladys. "Dad was probably working on the buoy house and took us kids for a walk to the dock."
Photograph courtesy of Gladys Meyer Davis

The Sheehan and Meyer families at Morris Island Light Station in 1933

Notice all the barefooted children in this family portrait of the Sheehans (mother Ellen Mary's family) and the Meyers. Keeper Edward Meyer, who is out of uniform for this relaxed occasion, is standing at the far right back of the group. "It was quite an accomplishment to get all our family members to and from the island!" remembers Gladys. The foundation of Morris Island Light Station is now permanently under water, and waves lap at the base of the lighthouse tower. Photograph courtesy of Gladys Meyer Davis

enjoy living at Ponce de Leon. "We played softball and hide-and-seek—with the best places a kid could ever want to hide! And we played jacks for hours on the concrete apron of the lighthouse," says Gladys. "We girls savored sitting on the keeper's porch playing with dolls and paper dolls. And how we loved to roller-skate. But we knew we'd better not go anywhere near the oleander and hibiscus that were planted in perfectly raked rows–it was strictly taboo to do anything that might cause a lighthouse inspector to make a negative remark about the light station, which directly reflected on us, the keepers and families. We never knew when the lighthouse inspector might show up." Even young Gladys knew how important it was for her father to get good reports from the inspector so he could keep his job during the Depression.

The family enjoyed generator-produced electricity, running water from an artesian well (installed in 1907), and indoor plumbing–a real luxury. "The children's job was to be sure to notify Father when the water tank was full. The tank was filled each evening by an electric pump installed in the late 1930s. This sulfur well water was used primarily in the bathroom."

Rainwater was collected through rain gutters that had to be opened when it started to rain to clean out the piping and then closed to gather the water. The rainwater ran under the house to a cistern. From there it was coaxed up to the kitchen and laundry area by hand pumps. "The laundry area was 'out back' in a shed. Mama eventually got a gasoline washing machine," says Gladys.

"The old privy was made of beautiful brick and served not as a bathroom but as a play-actors' dressing room from which we emerged the most famous actors who ever graced a stage. We really thought we were something, acting out our self-written, directed, and performed dramas. I remember a time when all five of us kids had to sit in the Chair as punishment following what we thought was the most ingenious of props. My brothers had burned matches to smudge our faces like makeup, but Father had another opinion of our resourcefulness!" Matches were one of a keeper's most important possessions–and were protected with a bulldog's conviction–in the days when the lighthouse kerosene lamp had to be lit each night.

"We did a lot of fishing from the lighthouse dock," Gladys continues, "and all five of us children would go swimming in the nearby river. My brothers kept the beach raked clear of oyster shells. While we splashed and pulled at each other and played water tag, Mother sat nearby under the big oak tree and did her sewing, keeping watch to make sure her brood was safe." Gladys chuckles when she recalls that her mother couldn't swim. "She would just look very serious and yell at us if we got too far from shore."

Gladys smiles when she thinks about her mother's cooking. "I can still smell her wonderful muffins," she declares. "During my childhood days at the lighthouse, seafood was very plentiful. If my father decided he would like to have fish or shrimp for supper, he would take the boat out in the river and catch all he needed in a short period of time. The waters were not polluted at that time, and there were fish and shrimp year-round and crabs, clams, and oysters in season. All were in great abundance.

"The highlight and social event of the day was when the mail arrived," Gladys continues. "The post office for Ponce Park, which was the name of this area at the time, was about two hundred feet from the lighthouse. Everyone knew about when Mr. Barker would arrive with the prized news and gathered early to do a little visiting."

Mr. Barker moonlighted as an ice delivery man, and he would grocery shop for the families for fifty cents and deliver the merchandise along with the mail. Gladys did a little entrepreneuring herself. "The postmistress at Ponce Park, Mrs. Gertrude Ryan, would hire me to tidy up her house." For her efforts, Gladys earned ten cents, which she often used to buy a cold drink from Mrs. Gertrude. "I would turn around and give the dime back to her for a Coca-Cola," laughs Gladys.

Turning more serious, Gladys says, "There were many times that I realized how important the lighthouse was. I can remember several times when a boat would wreck at the inlet. My father would rescue those on board and bring them to the lighthouse, where they would be given dry clothes and my mother would prepare meals for them."

All the Meyer children pitched in to help their father and mother. "Each evening Jack and Edward would ascend the seemingly endless stairs and take down the curtains that protected the lens. We girls were expected to help keep the house spotless. And I am still a meticulous housekeeper, having been ingrained with the fact that cleanliness was a must. A surprise visit from the lighthouse inspector brought tension because the dwelling and buildings had to be white-glove clean. Even today when I start doing housework my husband, Earl, tells me, 'The inspector is not coming today!' "

It was at Ponce de Leon that Gladys's brother Edward helped read the tide gauges. "He was paid a monthly salary to read and report his recordings, and this experience later counted toward his retirement from

Mrs. O'Neil (a family friend from New York), Jack and Edward, Mrs. O'Neil's daughter, Gladys, and Betty at Jupiter Inlet in 1932

Gladys and her sister and brothers sat on the steps of the double keepers' house with some guests from New York. It was always an event to have visitors, especially family members. Family time and play were top priorities for the Meyers. Photograph courtesy of Gladys Meyer Davis the U.S. Army Corps of Engineers," says Gladys.

"In 1939 the U.S. Coast Guard took over the U.S. Lighthouse Service, and in 1941, when the war started, the keepers' families had to move from Ponce de Leon Light Station and the homes were converted to barracks to house the coast guard personnel. It was then that my father purchased a house in Ponce Park so we children could attend school and the family could stay together. This is the same house that I live in today with my husband, Earl, and this is where we raised our two daughters, Julia and Ellen."

Julia is now in Laguna Beach, California, in the wine business, and sister Ellen is in her thirteenth year in the coast guard as a boatswain mate first class. Ellen was stationed at Dry Tortugas Lighthouse, where fifty years earlier her grandfather, Gladys's father, had served as lighthouse keeper. Gladys knows Keeper Edward Meyer would be very proud to know his granddaughter climbed the very steps he did to check on the light.

"I shall never forget my happy childhood memories of living at the lighthouses," concludes Gladys. "It was a wonderful time of family life, and as time goes by, we all cherish those times even more."

Gladys's strong bond with Ponce de Leon Light Station is evident as she continues to live within a shadow's distance of the lighthouse. She and her husband have worked hard for its preservation, with Gladys serving on the lighthouse advisory board and Earl serving as the treasurer of the preservation association. Recently Gladys donated her family's oak table and chairs, the ones they used throughout her father's career, to be used as part of the Ponce de Leon Inlet Lighthouse restoration. In honor of her years of persistent work for the restoration of the light station, the preservation association has named the building she was born in the Gladys Meyer Davis House. And so the circle of family life remains unbroken.

FAMILY RECIPE

Gladys says her family caught the fish for this recipe from the dock at whichever light station they happened to be living in at the time. Her mother always fried the cakes in a black iron pan.

MAMA'S FISH CAKES

4 medium white potatoes, peeled
About 1 pound whiting, bass, or sheephead
1 medium onion, finely diced
1 large egg
Salt and pepper to taste
$^1/_2$ cup shortening

Boil potatoes and mash. Cook fish in enough water to cover until done; when cool enough to handle, remove bones and separate into flakes. Combine flaked fish and mashed potatoes. Add onion, egg, salt, and pepper. Shape fish mixture into cakes, and fry in hot shortening until brown and crisp.

PONCE DE LEON INLET LIGHT STATION (renamed Ponce Inlet in 1963) was decommissioned in 1970 and relit in 1983 when it was once again needed due to the changing coastal building construction. The light station has been meticulously restored by the private, nonprofit Ponce de Leon Lighthouse Preservation Association.

From Daytona Beach take Florida Highway A1A south through Port Orange and straight onto the paved, unnumbered road that continues south through Wilbur-by-the-Sea to Ponce Inlet. (The "No Outlet" sign means you are on the right road.) The lighthouse is visible from several miles away, and the complex includes an outstanding gift/bookstore and displays in the keepers' homes, one of which has been named the Gladys Meyer Davis House. One of the restored buildings houses the original, still-working, first-order Fresnel lens from Cape Canaveral Lighthouse. The Ponce de Leon Inlet Light Station restoration offers one of the best experiences a lighthouse admirer can ever hope for, and the climb to the top of the lighthouse tower enhances the feel of serving in the U.S. Lighthouse Service in its heyday. For more information call 368/761-1821.

JUPITER INLET LIGHT STATION is off US 1, and the lighthouse tower, which is painted bright red, can be seen from the Loxahatchee River Bridge in Jupiter. Take the US 1 exit off I-95, go north for 1 mile, cross Indiantown Road, and turn right at the sign to Burt Reynolds Park. The light station, part of Jupiter Lighthouse Park, includes a small museum and a gift shop; all proceeds go to The Florida History Center and Museum, the nonprofit organization that maintains the light station. The light station is open Saturday through Wednesday from 10 a.m. to 3:15 p.m.; there is a nominal fee to climb the tower. For more information call 561/747-6639. The lighthouse and museum are located in Lighthouse Park. Maintenance and educational tours of the Jupiter Inlet Lighthouse are under the auspices of the Loxahatchee River Historical Society. Contact the society at 561/747-8380.

BODIE ISLAND

HOME IS WHERE THE LIGHTHOUSE IS

Joseph Lee Gaskill, Vernon Gaskill's father, served at the old Bodie Island Life-saving Station in the late 1800s. Keeping with his family's tradition of serving in life-saving and lighthouse service, Vernon joined the U.S. Lighthouse Service and accepted his first assignment as keeper of Hilton Head Range Light in South Carolina in 1912. Keeper Gaskill continued his distinguished career at Cape Romaine (South Carolina), Pamlico Point and Long Shoal Lights (North Carolina), and Craig Hill (Baltimore, Maryland) before filling the vacancy left by Ephraim "Capt. Eef" Meekins at Bodie Island in 1919. Shortly after the U.S. Coast Guard absorbed the lighthouse service in 1939, Vernon Gaskill, like many of the other 2,500 keepers (about half of the lighthouse keeper force), transferred into the coast guard as a boatswain mate first class.

The coast guard assigned Keeper Gaskill to the buoy tender depot in Coinjock, North Carolina, a position that carried a tremendous amount of responsibility. His new military rating didn't take into account Keeper Gaskill's thirty years of experience as a lightkeeper, but he continued to serve his country with dedication until his retirement at Coinjock Depot on January 1, 1948.

Keeper Vernon Gaskill Sr. and his wife, Bertha Davis Gaskill, had four children: Vernon Jr., John, Dorothy, and Erline. John and his two sisters share their memories of living at Bodie Island Light Station.

John Gaskill, second-oldest son of the principal keeper at Bodie Island Light Station, remembers seeing an aura of peachblow in the eastern sky over Bodie Island many summer mornings when he was a youngster. His father would wake him up about a half hour before sunrise and tell him it was time to snuff the flame in the lighthouse lamp. John also remembers trying to talk his father into letting him sleep just a few minutes longer–and his father's unrelenting reply. "No, John. To the top of the lighthouse, and note the exact time. Now get on with your job or the inspector is liable to check this station today for sure." That threat always got action from John who, much as he wanted to enjoy his vacation from school, understood the consuming work a keeper and his assistants faced as caretakers of a first-order light station.

Bodie Island Light Station in the early 1900s

A classic-style coastal lighthouse, Bodie Island Lighthouse has a granite foundation, brick walls, and marble floors. The oil-storage entry houses two workrooms separated by a central hallway; granite steps at the end of the hallway lead up to the spiral iron steps of the tower. The southside workroom has shelves with indentations designed to hold drums of oil. "These were not used as long as I was living here," says keeper's son John Gaskill. "A separate oil-storage building stood at the southeastern corner of the tower." Photograph courtesy of John Gaskill

At twelve and a half years of age John felt mature because his daddy trusted him to climb the 216 winding steps of the lighthouse, extinguish the lamp, and draw the curtains in the lantern room. He also felt proud to be following in the steps of other keepers at one of the most important lights on the East Coast. Mariners depended on the powerful first-order Fresnel lens at Bodie Island Lighthouse to send a 19-nautical-mile guiding spear of light into the dark gap between Currituck Beach Light Station to the north and Cape Hatteras to the south.

Until the early 1900s Bodie Island required a principal keeper as well as first and second assistants, with two of the three men on duty at all times. For more than thirty years the three keepers assigned to Bodie Island had sent numerous requests to the lighthouse authorities to expand the existing Double Keepers' Quarters to house all three men and their families, but the officials repeatedly denied the request. And since there was no school on Bodie Island, the keepers' children stayed on the mainland for most of the year, which meant many miles and weeks usually separated a keeper from his family.

John explains that in the 1920s the U.S. Lighthouse Service installed a thermostat over the lighthouse lamp to "watch" the flame, and this "mechanical keeper" eliminated the need for the second assistant keeper. The thermostat was linked to a warning bell in the keepers' dwelling and also to a recording device, similar to a seismograph. Although the thermostat cut back on the amount of time the remaining two keepers spent checking the flame when the lamp was lit, they still had to strain the oil through a piece of

The original first-order Fresnel lens at Bodie Island Lighthouse

Two 1,000-watt bulbs, a primary bulb and a backup, now illuminate the first-order Fresnel lens at Bodie Island Lighthouse. Although electric bulbs replaced the original incandescent oil vapor (IOV) lamp in the early 1930s, the lens is the same one that has focused sharp spears of light since 1872. The open cathedral-like interior of the Fresnel lens helped make it the most successful optic used by the U.S. Lighthouse Service because it accommodated both whale oil and kerosene lamps as well as electric bulbs. This particular lens was manufactured in Paris, disassembled, and shipped to Bodie Island, where it was reassembled like a puzzle. Original first-order Fresnel lenses are rare today.

chamois to ensure the least impurities and a clean-burning, bright flame and to make sure the lamp was properly lit. This eliminated the need for an assistant, and from then on, one keeper kept a lone vigil at Bodie Island Light Station. The lighthouse inspector always checked the thermostat's recording device for evidence of erratic burning, which meant a negative report on the keepers. In 1932 the U.S. Lighthouse Service replaced the oil lamp with an electric one.

One of the biggest jobs in maintaining a lighthouse is painting the tower, and in 1934 Keeper Vernon Gaskill asked the U.S. Lighthouse Service for permission to hire local labor to do the job. Depression had hit area fishing communities, and Keeper Gaskill wanted to help pump some money back into the area—as well as get the work done as quickly and easily as possible. Permission granted, Earl Mann—the son of the manager of the Bodie Island hunt club, Fritz Haymen, and eighteen-year-old John got the job.

As John puts it, it was not a job for the weak-hearted. The "paintbox" was attached on both sides by "falls," ropes on hooks connected to the stanchions of the catwalk railing. Every morning the three painters hoisted the box up the outside of the tower and

then climbed over the railing and down the falls into the box. Armed with scrapers, paintbrushes, and the black and white paint they had mixed with zinc, lead, linseed oil, and turpentine—and as much courage as they could muster, the three men scraped and painted. "Starting at the top of the tower we worked our way down—scrape,

Keeper Vernon Gaskill, wearing his work uniform, with Erline, his youngest daughter, and George Mann

John says that his father loved children and welcomed them anytime, even in the middle of his busy workday. George's brother, Max, and John spent a lot of time together fishing, hunting, and getting into mischief on this relatively isolated island. Photograph courtesy of John Gaskill

paint, lower the box; scrape, paint, lower the box, and so on and on and *on*. We had to keep one eye on the weather, and if it even looked like rain, we couldn't paint."

To paint the area under the catwalk, John put the ends of a board into the holes of the massive iron braces to make a scaffolding. Serious acrobatics–"but we loved the work," says John with a smile. "We were getting three dollars a day! Normal pay would have been only a dollar a day." John is still powerful-proud of his accomplishment but has kept his vow to never do anything like it again. Looking up the tall tower today, he laughs with disbelief that he even attempted painting it.

John and his friend Max found other, tamer ways to earn money too. "Once a year the buoy tender came to deliver supplies like paint, wood, and coal," John explains. "It was hard to transfer the supplies because the tender came

Principal Keeper Vernon Gaskill Sr. with Dixie, one of his favorite Chesapeake Bay retrievers

Dixie accompanied Keeper Gaskill everywhere except the tower. She would walk with him on his morning routine around the light station but would stop at the tower door. When he finished preparing the lamp for the next evening and came back down, Dixie would be there to greet him. Photograph courtesy of John Gaskill

into the sound through Stetson Channel, between Duck and Roanoke Islands, and would run aground. The crew would have to haul the supplies some distance by hand to the landing. One summer Max and I earned money by picking up the supplies at the landing and getting them to the lighthouse. It was a job! Whoever got the contract to haul the supplies had to have a horse and cart, and the only horse on Bodie Island was the one owned by the hunt club. Max's father ran the club and let us borrow the horse so we could get the job.

"When we were younger, say eleven and twelve years old, we got even more fun when the supplies were delivered. The supplies came in nice, reinforced boxes, and we'd use them for the bodies of wagons. For the wheels, we'd beat blocks off the wreck of the schooner *Laura A. Barnes*, beached in front of the lighthouse in 1921, to get the pulley wheels and add them to homemade wood axles. The wagons didn't last long, but we didn't care–anything to distract us for a while.

"In the early days, from say 1919 until the bridge to Roanoke Island was completed around 1928, the closest town was Elizabeth City, forty miles away. The mail came in by the steamer *Trenton* to Manteo. Someone was hired by the postal service to pick it up and take it to Wanchese by horse and cart. To get our mail, Daddy had to make the three-mile trip across Pamlico Sound to Wanchese," says John.

"Our family had to supply our own food," he continues. "I remember Mama buying canned corned beef by the case to take over to the island with us each summer. Compared to others during the Depression, we had it good. As a kid I didn't notice right away though—we didn't have money to spend anyway. We salted drum, spot, mullet, and herring for the winter. I do remember in 1934 when fishermen would find big schools of fish. Before hauling the fish in, though, we would hurry into town to ask the local fish buyer if he wanted to buy what we caught. Sometimes during those hard times the buyer could not afford to pay us."

U.S. Lighthouse Service jobs were coveted during the Depression, and Vernon Gaskill held the esteemed principal keeper's position at a very important lighthouse, with top pay at $140 a month. "Daddy paid $20 a month rent on the keepers' quarters on Bodie Island, so his pay was $120 a month," John says—and he has all his father's records to back up these numbers.

John and his two sisters, Dorothy and Erline, have vivid memories of the lighthouse inspectors who visited Bodie Island. "The word went out from Baltimore as soon as the lighthouse tender left port. Everything had to shine—and you'd better not even put a hand on a doorknob! It was the only time Daddy wore his uniform. Boy, things got hot! Everything was scrubbed and painted," John says with a serious laugh. "And we kids just kind of made ourselves scarce."

During the school year the Gaskill kids lived at the family home in Wanchese, with an addition to the main part of the house having been built from salvaged lumber from the shipwrecked *Laura A. Barnes*. John recalls, "School was out May 20th, and we'd leave as soon as we could for Bodie Island. We'd each carry all we possibly could down to Davis Landing, south of Wanchese. We'd load everything into the lighthouse powerboat, cross the sound, draw near the lighthouse through the creeks, and transfer everything to a skiff to haul it to the keepers' quarters. Sometimes the assistant keeper would be waiting, and almost before we could get off the boat, he was headed back to the mainland. Sometimes the mosquitoes were so thick we would be breathing them. And with our arms loaded, we didn't have a free hand to swat at 'em!"

Dorothy adds, "And the gnats! Sometimes they'd even come through the screens. We'd have to close the windows and swelter!"

"The gnats always came with an east wind. I never understood why," John comments.

Each summer the lighthouse family moved into the south side of the keepers' duplex living quarters. If the assistant and his family were gone and the Gaskills had company, they'd often exchange or share the other half of the house. And if Keeper Vernon Gaskill was on duty during Christmas week, the family would again pack up a boat and reunite with their father at the lighthouse. "It really wasn't any different," John comments. "Christmas was just another time we sometimes went to Bodie Island to all be together. I don't remember having a tree or anything. And there weren't many gifts. We were just together."

Dorothy visualizes traveling to the lighthouse in the days when the family had a Chevy sedan and the bridge to Roanoke Island had been built. "There we were–a carload of kids, clothes and food, dogs and cats moving to the lighthouse. We raised Chesapeake Bay retrievers, and one of them liked to ride on the running board. We'd go flying over the sand ruts to the beach and onto the firmer flats north of the coast guard station. That dog would jump off to chase a rabbit and get back on, but he never fell off! One male we had sat on a watermelon all the way."

John remembers Chess, one of the retrievers who would go up every morning to put out the light with him. "That dog would climb every step with me, but he wouldn't enter the lantern room. Maybe it was the smell of the kerosene burning that stopped him."

John and his sisters also remember some of the mischief they got into, especially at the pond in front of the lighthouse. John and older brother Vernon Jr. loved to coax Dorothy into their small boat. No matter how many times they promised not to overturn the boat, they always did. Dorothy tells of one summer day when the Gaskills were expecting company. Since visitors were few and far

John Gaskill in his U.S. Navy uniformin 1935
John Gaskill says, "I used to go on the balcony and follow the ships, sometimes sailing ships in those days, from horizon to horizon and dream of all the places they were headed." When he was old enough, John joined the U.S. Navy. "In the days of the Depression, that was a dream come true. Man was I excited!" says John. Photograph courtesy of John Gaskill

PROBATIONARY APPOINTMENT

Department of Commerce and Labor
APPOINTMENT DIVISION
Washington

April 5, 1912.

Mr. Lloyd V. Gaskill,

    Through the Commissioner of Lighthouses.

Sir:

    You have been appointed, subject to taking the oath of office,

_____ Assistant Keeper _____

in the _____ Lighthouse Service _____

at a salary of _____ Four Hundred and Eighty _____ dollars

                             or entered

per ___annum___, effective on the date on which you enter/_____ upon

duty in the above-mentioned position.

    (By selection from certificate No. _____, and subject to a
probationary period of not to exceed six months as provided by
paragraph (c) of section 1 of civil-service rule VII, to be found
on the reverse hereof.)

Reported for duty, April 21, 1912

By direction of the Secretary:

    Respectfully,

        G. W. Kennedy
        Chief of Appointment Division.

Appropriation: Salaries, Keepers of Lighthouses.
Vice: Edward Simmons.
Legal Residence: North Carolina.

between, this was a special occasion. All of the kids had on their best clothes. "I can recall exactly what I had on that day," Dorothy chuckles, "a pink-and-white checked dress and black-patent Mary Jane's. Mama told me not to DARE go near the pond and get messed up. Well somehow John and Vernon Jr. got me down to the pond and into the boat they had built and right into the water. Mama was so mad. John, Vernon, and I got a switching!"

"We kids got into a lot of trouble sometimes out there at the lighthouse because there wasn't much to do but fish and swim," adds John. "Our chores kept us busy enough though. Just when you were through with one job, it was time to start over. We had to keep our jobs done so we could fit in swimming, fishing, and beachcombing."

Dorothy adds, "We used to climb over the railing [of the catwalk] and walk on the ledge–six or seven inches wide at the most–and lean out hanging onto the railing. Of course this was without our parents' knowledge!"

"Of course, we did it on the side away from the house so Mama and Daddy couldn't see us," John interjects.

"I even remember John standing on the ventilator ball and leaning against the lightning rod! Can you believe he is affected by heights now? And Erline doesn't like elevators or bridges," Dorothy reveals.

Bodie Island seems to have an affinity for lightning. According to one story, the lightning rod originally was grounded to the stairway. A keeper was on the stairs when a bolt hit, and he was temporarily paralyzed. The lightning rod was then attached to the outside of the tower. About 1939 a rogue lightning bolt hit the tower, ran along the ground, entered the keepers' quarters by way of the telephone line, and scared the life

out of Erline. "I remember playing at the top of the stairs and seeing glass shattering. The telephone flew off the wall and burned, and balls of lightning rolled across the stairs. I ran halfway down the stair, jumped into Mama's arms and then into Daddy's. I was worried about my kitten burning," she says.

John and Erline Gaskill at Bodie Island Light Station in the late 1930s
Proud sister Erline stands with her older brother, John, who was home on leave from the navy. During the 1930s, Erline and Assistant Keeper Julian Austin's children were among the few children to reside full-time at Bodie Island Light Station. Isolation, lack of a school and church, and not enough living space made the island less than ideal for families. Photograph courtesy of John Gaskill

John Gaskill tries on his father's uniform for size

"I thought about becoming a keeper," John says in his quiet manner. "But after the summer when I painted the lighthouse, I decided to go join the ships I watched with envy. I would sit out on the catwalk and play my guitar–so I wouldn't disturb anybody. I knew I'd be on a ship in time." Photograph courtesy of John Gaskill

"I love stormy weather," John says emphatically. "The ocean roaring and the wind drawing and whistling in and around the lighthouse was exciting when I was a kid. I could hear the surf–Boom! and it meant good hunting along the beach. It was always exciting to see what washed up after a good storm. I still like a good old nor'easter to this day. It reminds me of when I was young and lived at the lighthouse."

The Gaskill kids got to take tourists up into the tower sometimes, and they always hoped for a tip. A quarter was what they needed for a movie and popcorn in Manteo. Erline also knew that she had to pick exactly ten quarts of blackberries at 2¢ a quart to earn a movie ticket.

When Erline and her mother moved to Bodie Island in 1937 to be with Keeper Gaskill year-round, Erline's older brothers and sister had struck out on their own, and for the next three years she was the only Gaskill child living on the island. "I remember one especially lonely day at the lighthouse. I watched Daddy napping on the couch in the living room for a while, and then I went up to him and said, 'Daddy, take me fishing.' He smiled and said, 'Certainly.' He took me to the pier near the creek by the hunting club, where all us children used to fish and swim together."

Since there was no paved road between the lighthouse and Wanchese at the time, Keeper Gaskill drove Erline to Whalebone Junction every school morning at 7 o'clock to catch the bus. For the Gaskills and other children who grew up at light stations, lack of communication with the outside world often caused problems when they went to a new school where almost all the other children had grown up together. Erline was twelve years younger than her brother John and she felt timid when she first went to Manteo School in the fourth grade. "I soon got over it though and made good friends," she says.

Erline loved to read, and having a new library open in Manteo provided books that helped her transcend her loneliness.

"I'll tell you how isolated Bodie Island was," Dorothy goes on. "When I was a teenager and received punishment, my parents made me spend a weekend in the winter at Bodie Island. Even so, Daddy was my hero."

Some people think keepers were social misfits, loners, or recluses, but Lloyd Vernon Gaskill Sr. disproves that misperception. "Until Daddy was ninety years old he rented rooms of his home in Wanchese to visitors who couldn't find anywhere else to stay. He was a wonderful person," says Dorothy. "I wish you could have met him. His philosophy was 'Every morning when I wake up, it's a brand new day because it's one I didn't expect to have.' He was so outgoing and thoroughly enjoyed meeting people. One couple spent their honeymoon in our family home. They thought so much of him they stayed in touch with him until he passed away."

"We went through a lot to be a family at the lighthouse," Dorothy continues, "but I will never forget the most beautiful sunsets from the top of the light and running up and down the lighthouse steps and thinking nothing of it. It was worth it."

Keeper Vernon Gaskill Sr. started his U.S. Lighthouse Career at Hilton Head Range Light in South Carolina in 1912 and served at Cape Romaine (South Carolina), Pamlico Point and Long Shoal Lights (North Carolina), and Craig Hill (near Baltimore, Maryland) before filling the vacancy left by Ephraim "Capt. Eef" Meekins at Bodie Island Light Station in 1919. Shortly after the coast guard absorbed the lighthouse service in 1939, Vernon Gaskill and some 2,500 other keepers transferred into the coast guard with the military title boatswain mate first class. The coast guard assigned Keeper Gaskill to the buoy tender depot in Coinjock, North Carolina, and gave him tremendous responsibility. His new military title didn't take into account his thirty years of experience, but Vernon Gaskill Sr. continued to serve his country with dedication.

"At Coinjock he relieved Bill James Tate, the man who had housed the Wright Brothers during their test flights," John remembers. "Daddy had a great deal of responsibility with this assignment. He had to go up to Currituck Beach Light at least once a week to check the light, plus he had to tend beacons and other aids to navigation for a big area."

"How happy I was when Daddy transferred to Coinjock," Erline says. The small town of Coinjock was a virtual metropolis compared to Bodie Island. Boaters would alert Keeper Gaskill about any problems, and Erline remembers going with her father on late-night trips along North Landing River to tend the 2-foot-high post lanterns that had gone out. She recalls sleeping on the deck of the boat and feeling the cold spray on her face and seeing the glow of Norfolk lights on the horizon.

Boats, even big barges and U.S. PT boats, often used the intercoastal waterway that flowed right up to the front door of Coinjock Depot. From 1941 to '42 many mariners, including American PT boat crews, used the waterway to avoid encountering German U-boats along the Atlantic Coast. Dorothy recalls a night in 1942 when she served coffee to John Kennedy, then a young PT boat officer. About 11:30 there was a lot of noise at the dock, and when Keeper Gaskill went to check, the PT boat crew asked him for coffee. " 'Dot,' I heard Daddy call, 'make these fellas some coffee.' And so I served coffee to a very famous man."

In 1996 the three surviving Gaskill children visited Bodie Island Light Station together for the first time since the 1930s. They went to the visitor's center in the original double keepers' dwelling and entered the door on the south side of the building. When the Gaskill family lived in the house, they kept the case holding the U.S. Lighthouse Service traveling library on the floor near the back door. "Daddy read everything in that library. It contained all sorts of books," John explains

The door that now enters the exhibit area once opened to the assistant keeper's quarters. "When Bodie Island Lighthouse was a manned station, each side was sealed off from the other to give us privacy," John points out.

Their family kitchen now serves as the cash register area for the visitor's center. On the west wall is a window that once framed the old hand pump and sink, and in the center of the south wall is the fireplace where the cookstove was vented. John says, "My brother, Vernon Jr., and I spent many hours on the floor in front of the fire playing checkers. In the winter Daddy used a coal stove that was vented out the fireplace."

Keeper Gaskill's desk stood along the wall separating the living room from the kitchen. He kept his daily log and records here. Like every other keeper, Vernon Gaskill had to account for every item delivered to, consumed at, and removed from the light station. Keeper Gaskill also recorded the species of birds that flew migratory paths over Bodie Island.

The living room of the keepers' duplex now houses a bookstore, and on the wall at the foot of the stairs leading to the second floor were the barometer and the telephone, the only connection with the outside world and only to be used to report to other keepers and to the staffs of area life-saving stations. "We kids slept in the bedroom to the left at the top of the stairs. Mama and Daddy had the bedroom down the hall," John says. "I remember Daddy's chest of drawers. You know what was kept in the top drawer? Not clothes—no, much, much more important things—matches to light the lamp and chamois skins and towels for cleaning the lens."

There was an extra room at the top of the stairs. "Daddy had made request after request for a bathtub, and the lighthouse service finally agreed. Water was pumped from

(From left) Erline, Dorothy, "Mama" Bertha, Vernon Jr., Vernon Sr., and John at the Gaskill family home in Wanchese in 1941
The Gaskill family home on Roanoke Island is just across Pamlico Sound from Bodie Island Light Station. Photograph courtesy of John Gaskill

the cistern to fill the tub, and Daddy got in and almost froze to death. Since we had no warm water readily available, it was the last time he used the bathtub!" John says.

"That room became my playroom after Mama and I came here to stay year-round with Daddy," Erline comments. "I always had a kitten and a book to keep me company in that room." It was also where the U.S. Lighthouse Service-issued medicine chest was stored.

In 1932 the U.S. Lighthouse Service electrified the lighthouse tower but not the double keepers' dwelling. "Electricity eventually came to our house, but we used lamps in each room when I first moved there when I was eight years old," Erline remembers.

Going out the back door toward the tower, John points to the cement platform on the southeast side of the house. "A woodshed the government built used to stand there. Daddy told them not to leave it open without doors, that the first hurricane would take it out—and it did. The rest of it is somewhere over in the marsh."

He then points to a spot about a hundred feet from the house. "That's where the out-

Keeper Vernon Gaskill Sr. in 1984 at age 94
"I wish you could have known Daddy,"
daughter Dorothy fondly says of her
"Paps." "He was a kind man who knew
no stranger." Photograph courtesy of
John Gaskill

door bathroom was and a storage house. Each side of the keepers' house had its own privy." Sweeping his arm and pointing to the land surrounding the lighthouse, John comments, "I kept the yard mowed. There wasn't as much grass as now, but it was plenty big for a young boy. And it was a push mower—it weighed as much as I did!" How long did it take? "Oh, about the time I was finished, it was time to start over," John laughs.

"You know, a lighthouse isn't like a ship that can be taken to shore and repaired," John notes. "The U.S. Lighthouse Service had to bring in work parties—blacksmiths, metal-smiths, and carpenters. It was often busy here."

Dorothy and Erline talk about their pas-times at the light station. "We used to hunt for turtle eggs, just for fun," Dorothy chuckles.

"Yes! That's right," Erline continues. "And we'd look for something on the ground in the shape of a horseshoe. And then we'd dig for treasure."

"We'd take a coal bucket and go down to George's Creek, which we leased from the county, and get oysters. They got heavy!" adds John, who has the original 1903 Dare County deed showing the purchase of the oyster bed from Mr. Blevins.

Walking down the original 1870 brick walkway to the lighthouse, John continues, "Daddy would come out here about thirty minutes before sundown. He would go to the storage house that was outside the tower on the south side, fill a three-gallon brass can with oil, and get a bucket of coal. Next he would climb the stairs to the watch room, fill the oil reservoir, and watching the gauges carefully, pump the oil to pressurize it and send it upward into the mantle in the center of the Fresnel lens in the lantern room. Then Daddy would climb the stairs to the lantern room, go in, take the alcohol torch from its holder, light the torch, and use it to warm the kerosene to vaporize it. The kerosene vapor burned in the mantle, producing a brilliant light.

"The incandescent oil vapor lamp at Bodie Island was a great improvement over the old wick lamps. Daddy told me that before his time at the lighthouse there were five wick-burning lamps inside the lens, and the smoke and heat from the five lamps required a special shaft opening at the top canopy and the ventilator ball."

In the southside workroom of the lighthouse tower, John points to the small cement casing in the floor where the flash controller was located. "Bodie Island was a fixed, steady light until an electric light bulb replaced the IOV [incandescent oil vapor] lamp about 1932.

"And you know, there wasn't the problem with birds flying into the lantern after the light became flashing," John says. The flash controller gave Bodie Island light its distinctive alternating two and one-half seconds on, two and one-half seconds off in a thirty-second cycle.

Before the installation of the thermostat and warning bell in the keepers' dwelling, a keeper had to be in the watch room at all times when the lamp was lit. A warming stove kept the chill of wind and rain at bay for the keeper on duty. Bits of shaken-down coals are strewn around the tower's base, remnants of cold, lonely duty in the tower. Keeper Gaskill kept the first watch of each night, and the assistant keeper relieved him around midnight.

An octogenarian, John still climbs the stairs to the lantern room with ease. "I used to come up here with my dog and guitar. I'd go out on the balcony and play so I wouldn't disturb anybody. By the hour, I watched the ships going by, knowing one day I'd be on one of them, on my way 'round the world." Seafaring men go back many generations of Gaskills. "I definitely have salt in my veins."

John left his family at Bodie Island in 1933 and worked on the dredge *Chinook* out of Norfolk headed to the Gulf Coast. In the summer of '34 he returned to Bodie Island to paint the lighthouse, and in December he joined the navy. "In the days of the Depression, that was a dream come true. Man, was I excited!"

John completed his basic training in Norfolk before being sent to the West Coast, and he witnessed action during World War II from the deck of the battleship *Washington*.

John concludes, "Daddy almost always got the Star of Efficiency from the lighthouse inspector."

Shading her eyes as she looks upward at the stately Bodie Island tower, Dorothy emphasizes, "This lighthouse must be restored and saved. There's so much history here for people to learn."

Erline wraps it up when she says, "To lose it would be a shame. This country needs history for children to learn of their past and feel a sense of duty and identity."

FAMILY RECIPES

Mrs. Gaskill often served boiled drum for breakfast, although it was welcome at any meal. The fish were caught, cleaned, cut into large pieces, layered with salt, and kept in a wooden barrel or pottery crock filled with saltwater. John explains, "After supper we would get several pieces of drum out of the saltwater, bring them in, and wash them off. Then we'd put them in a big dishpan to soak in freshwater—Mama knew how long the fish had been in the brine and sometimes would change the water at bedtime. The next morning we'd pull the fish out of the freshwater and boil it on the wood stove with potatoes. If we really needed filling up, Mama cooked more potatoes. We put fatback drippings on the fish—bacon has a taste of its own, but fatback just makes the drum taste its best." (Darrell's, a restaurant in Manteo, serves boiled drum every Monday.)

John adds, "And we always had biscuits. Every morning, Mama made a big plate of them."

MAMA'S BISCUITS

¼ cup lard
2 cups flour
About ¾ cup water (a little more or less, according to the amount of flour)
Pinch of salt

Work the lard into the dough. (John says that if his mother had cracklings—the crisp, brown skin from frying fatback—she'd work them into the dough too.) Add the water and salt, and knead the dough lightly.
Pinch off pieces of the dough and hand-roll them into biscuits. Place the biscuits in a greased iron skillet and bake at 425° for about 12 to 15 minutes.

Not having refrigeration until the 1940s, Mrs. Gaskill often relied on canned foods to feed her family. "I've had canned corned beef about every way you can imagine," laughs John Gaskill.

CANNED CORNED BEEF WITH POTATOES

5 cups potatoes, diced
1 (12 oz.) can corned beef, flaked
1 large onion, chopped
Salt and pepper to taste
Water

Place the diced potatoes, flaked corned beef, chopped onion, salt, and pepper into a large pot. Cover with water, and boil until the potatoes are done.

BODIE ISLAND LIGHT STATION, in Cape Hatteras National Seashore, is visible from North Carolina Highway 12 after entering the national seashore. Turn right at the Bodie Island Visitors Center sign. The grounds are open year-round. The National Park Service provides interpretive programs and guided climbing tours of the restored lighthouse. The lighthouse is open for climbing from Easter through Columbus Day weekend. The Double Keepers' Quarters houses a bookstore, exhibits, and a visitors center that is open daily usually from 9 a.m. until 5 p.m. with hours extended to 6 p.m. during summer. For more information, including climbing reservations, call 252/475-9417.

OUTER ISLAND
MEMORIES, POEMS, AND PAINTINGS

In April 1935 the U.S. Lighthouse Service assigned Alva G. Carpenter to Outer Island Light Station, on one of the twenty-two Apostle Islands in Lake Superior off the coast of Wisconsin. After more than five years of faithful service at this remote outpost, Keeper Carpenter transferred to Raspberry Island, another of the six light stations in the Apostle chain. In 1944, five years after the U.S. Coast Guard took control of America's lighthouses, Keeper Carpenter was assigned to a station on the Michigan mainland because of his failing health.

Keeper Alva Carpenter and his wife, Marie, had three children: Fran and her much younger sister Lucy (born on Outer Island in 1938) and brother Frank (born on Raspberry Island in 1941). Fran cried when she said good-bye to her third-grade classmates in Minnesota and crossed the thirty miles of Lake Superior waters to her lighthouse home on Outer Island, Wisconsin. Before long, though, her heart belonged to this northeasternmost of the Apostle Islands, a love she now expresses in poetry and watercolors. As a teenager, Fran lived on the Wisconsin mainland during the school year, at first staying with friends and later earning her room and board. She missed her parents and her island dearly, but as she notes, "Adversity has the effect of exciting talents that in prosperous circumstances would have lain dormant." The following excerpts from Fran's memoir recall her days as a keeper's daughter, first at Outer Island and later at Raspberry Island.

Fran's memoir begins, "On the opening page of my mother's old scrapbook there is a telegram now faded through the years, though its message is still legible. It states briefly, Alva G. Carpenter, c/o Keeper, Two Harbors Light Station, Two Harbors, Minnesota. Transfer Outer Island approved–relieve present keeper May 1st. It was signed F. P. Dillon, Superintendent of Lighthouses, and dated April 29, 1935, Detroit, Michigan.

"It takes little effort to recollect the chain of events that immediately followed. The next day our family of three began the long drive to Wisconsin, riding in a huge yellow-orange dray. I was seated on the rear of the flatbed among an array of crated boxes and bags and clinging to the small covered wire cage that held our hapless canary. We rumbled beneath the great old railroad overpass at the outskirts of Two Harbors,

Outer Island Light Station, Wisconsin

Fran Carpenter Platske has felt spiritually connected to Outer Island since her childhood days as the keeper's daughter—and she returns to the island every chance she gets. The two-story brick house her family lived in is connected to the lighthouse tower by an enclosed walkway. Italianate detailing on the 1874 white tower makes it one of the most beautiful lighthouses on the Great Lakes.

Minnesota. Silently I bade a sad farewell to my third-grade classmates.

"But an exciting and memorable chapter of my life was about to unfold. Soon I would forget my young friends as we approached Bayfield, Wisconsin, which would become my hometown forever.

"On the third day, now May 1st, 1935, daybreak brought with it bitter, cutting slices of cold Canadian north winds. Regardless of weather conditions, the second assistant keeper, who was anxiously awaiting our arrival, was insistent on departure. The voyage would be thirty-one miles into open seas in a twenty-six-foot government-owned launch. With all latched and secured we set out, the American flag flying gaily in the breeze from the stern deck. Dispelling any immediate thoughts of danger, the assistant keeper challenged the raging winds as we attempted crossing the treacherous northwest channel, the final leg of our journey.

"Gigantic waves swept over the cabin, the engine sputtered, and slow speed was essential. Constant use of the bilge pump was in order for fear of being swamped by each onslaught of icy waters. Portholes were sealed, creating a sickening odor of fumes expelled from the gray marine engine.

"Arriving at the island, I was too ill to lift my head from the locker where I lay. Still, this was not to be the end of our nightmarish voyage. Several approaches to the dock were made, but the tremendous force of wind and wave made unboarding impossible. The sturdy boat twisted and heaved as it was swung around in the trough and crest of the seas, positioned to seek safe shelter that the south end of Outer Island provided. A boat working in such tremendous seas is an awesome sight.

"With protection now from the furious winds, we lay anchored offshore throughout the night, riding out the gale in the dead roll of the sea. By morning Lake Superior had not yet surrendered. Hastily we managed to unboard at the foreboding high dock hoping the launch would not be slammed against its huge pilings. Having succeeded, we followed a somewhat overgrown path the assistant keeper had previously told us about. It would lead us to an abandoned old lumber camp. From there the path would lead us directly to the lighthouse. However, this path disappeared into overgrown wilderness and tall timber. We made the remainder of our way following the ice-studded shoreline and tangled masses of underbrush yet untouched by man.

"It was dusk when the first glimpse of Outer Island Lighthouse came into view across the bay. The beams from its tower were beginning to pierce the night. Unlike many other points of the island, this area grew a wealth of tall jack pines. An eagle's nest rested atop the tallest of them all. It was here Father removed his newly purchased coveralls, now badly tattered and torn, revealing his 'best dress' clothing beneath, and hung them on a branch of one of the jack pines. We went forth to meet the retiring keeper and his wife, Walter and Emma Daniels. They had been stationed there eighteen years. I was given a cup of warm, diluted canned milk and pillowed down behind an immense oil-burning space heater to warm my shivering body (an educated guess, we had walked approximately ten miles).

"An integral part of the lighthouse families' lives consisted of maintaining strict schedules and abiding by government rules and regulations. Most island stations were staffed by three men: the keeper and his first and second assistants. Once a month each man in turn was allowed a four-day leave of absence, returning with food, supplies, and mail. Each man took a four-hour watch: four on, four off. Fog, an incessant danger to Great Lakes vessels, demanded full-time vigilance. Warming the mantle and lighting the wick inside the Fresnel lens was an hour-long procedure and claimed priority, followed by close observance for exact and constant brilliance. Every four hours the immense cable that rotated the tower's third-order Fresnel lens needed rewinding.

"Summer months were filled with countless tasks. From the beach boathouse, fog signal on the cliff, dwellings, and small warehouses to the top of the towering lighthouse, nothing was left unpainted or unvarnished. Where stations had tall towers, men took to a scaffold with huge flat brushes and buckets of whitewash, inching their way from top to bottom, repeating until the conical tower and trim were complete.

"Mother, like most other wives, had the inevitable chores of washing clothes over tub and washboard, using flat irons for ironing, picking wild berries for canning, and always the dusting, sweeping, and scrubbing. The aroma of her homemade bread tempted us all to the kitchen.

"In the finale, near midsummer, the lighthouse tender *Amaranth* approached from the west. Through the binoculars one could see the American flag flying astern, and beneath it flew a smaller flag that indicated a government inspector was aboard. However there need be no fear of this yearly inspection–the station had been well managed. Upon departure the *Amaranth* belched forth a huge stream of black puffing smoke. The fog-signal engines were fired up. Each blasted a farewell salute, one to the other.

"It was during one of these annual inspections that I chose to venture out with my flat-bottom rowboat to the lighthouse tender. From shore it appeared a mere two or three blocks. Later I was told that a round trip was more like three miles, as distance on water is deceiving. The sea was calm, the air still. Vaguely sensing an oncoming summer squall, I gave no heed to nature's warning and proceeded forth on my new adventure. Approaching the huge ship in my wee boat, the sailors advised that I turn back immediately–a big wind was coming in from the southwest. Besides, I was not allowed aboard ship.

"Disappointed, I turned back. Blisters had already formed on my hands from rowing, but now I would have to row more vigorously. After completing a near half-circle I managed to lamely pull the boat ashore. By now the wind had whipped up the once-calm sea into a frothy foam. Climbing the tramway steps to the top, I was greeted by a very angry and scolding father. The captain of the tender, standing with his hands behind his back, said, 'We were watching over you and would have come to your rescue if you needed it!' It seemed to soothe my inner hurt as I walked solemnly away.

"I, too, had daily tasks, but if finished according to schedule, I would run to the one-room whitewashed log cabin near the end of the woods. This was my headquarters, my playhouse, my 'inner sanctum.'

"One bright sunny afternoon I stumbled on a grave marker. Parting the mass of weeds and overgrowth, I knelt to look at the carefully inscribed words in its weather-beaten wood. It read: 'Here lies my faithful dog Dick, died in 1906.' Imagining the burial scene, I walked away to wonder time and again about the dog and its master. Nature

Looking out the windows of the lantern room of Outer Island Lighthouse

Keeper Alva Carpenter kept a watchful eye on the busy shipping lanes of Lake Superior from the lighthouse lantern room at Outer Island, the northeasternmost of the twenty-two Apostle Islands. The U.S. Coast Guard has replaced the original third-order Fresnel lens with a plastic optic and has installed a solar-power source and automated controls. Outer Island Light Station no longer requires daily human hands, only a once-a-year check by coastguardsmen.

became my best friend. Watching the bald eagles through the powerful government binoculars was fascinating. How graceful and yet mighty were these enormous birds. Listening to the cry of the timber wolves filling the night air gave me a wistful feeling, or attempting an imitated answer to the laughing sound of the loons as they played underwater hide-and-seek. Somehow the squawking seagulls never really minded, I supposed. Roaming along the sparkling white sandy beaches, sometimes I would attempt to swim in the frigid waters.

"On occasion I would carry my old 'grandmother' pet hen with me and lay her down in a nest of green leaves beneath my favorite birch tree. She rested there until I was tired and had to go home. One summer a fox was encaged in the now-empty chicken coop. But no matter how I desired to pet him, he cowered in the shelter. Soon thereafter he dug his way under the fence and claimed his freedom as he disappeared into the night. Happy for him, I also missed his presence. Then it would be wild berry season.

Feasting on them, I also found hazelnut bushes. The squirrels chattered and scolded, but they never did come to my open hand for a morsel. The air was pure, as was the icy water, and I drank freely of both. Often at night I fell asleep watching the billions of stars twinkling down through my bedroom window and listening to the cry of a lone timber wolf. I felt in communion with him and nature.

"In spring, around April, when navigation opened on the Great Lakes, Father would bus to Duluth, Minnesota, where he and other offshore lighthouse keepers boarded a lighthouse tender to be taken to their prospective stations. Later Father would come to town in the launch and take Mother and me to the island. There we stayed until near the navigational closing of Great Lakes shipping. During the school year I remained in Bayfield, Wisconsin, first being boarded with friends, but in later years earning my keep.

"This became perhaps the only event of lighthouse living that was difficult. My very being craved to be on that beautiful island where I lived each cherished summer. But I had to get on with my schooling. Each time my parents came into Bayfield and then returned to the island after their four-day leave, I watched as the boat pulled away from the government slip and then quickly, I would race to the city dock, stand there and wave as it sailed by. Always the American flag waved gaily back from the stern deck. As fast as possible I would run through the village, up Cemetery Hill, and up the

firetower, a distance of approximately four miles. Climbing to its very top I would watch that little boat disappear out into the bay and into the first open channel. I knew my heart was always aboard. On a clear day, you can see forever–it is true.

"But there were many times in later years my spirits soared with delight and fervor as Father allowed me behind the steering wheel during a vehement storm while he maneuvered

Fran, her father, and the family dog on Outer Island about 1935

"This is my favorite picture of my dad and me," says Fran. "There was always a cold wind blowing!" Despite the cold, young Frannie is barefoot in this picture. Photograph courtesy of Fran Carpenter Platske

the engine. He had taught me how to crisscross through tunnels of enormous waves, and I was rather proud the day he let me steer the boat into the narrow boatways when waves were washing over the dock and cascading down the boathouse roof. Then there were the long trips in still, thick gray fog. We would watch for deadheads [logs and other floating debris], blow the horn intermittently, and listen for other boats that might appear ghostlike through the next fog bank. Now that I had been taught how to handle the wheel, it was time to learn to read a compass. It would be most easy to become lost among the islands or run ashore on a sandbar.

"There was one storm I recall in which I learned even more respect for my father's ability as a seagoing man, and that was the season he was to make the final trip into Bayfield to pick up the station's last food supply and mail before navigation closed. He told me that after he crossed the Northwest Channel a winter storm came bristling across Lake Superior from Canada. Reaching the bay hours later, fishermen had seen him enter the harbor. Their report was that the launch was listing heavily with thick sheets of glaring ice weighing it down. More frightening was the listing of the boat as it settled in the trough of each wave, heaving sideways as though gasping for a last breath, only to sink and rise to the crest of another crushing wave. Dockside, the fishermen assisted Father to a nearby fishhouse where his inch-thick ice-covered mackinaw stood on the fishhouse floor. His hands were badly frostbitten. The boat itself appeared as a shapeless iceberg. The portholes were covered with ice. The launch doors were opened only for seeing the path ahead, thus flooding the interior. It amazes me to this day how Father managed the engine, the side steering wheel, and the bilge pump and yet saw the chosen route ahead. Three days later, the remaining men on Outer Island Light Station received their mail and additional foods. The keeper—my Father—had returned.

"I take pause at the typewriter to honor here all those seagoing men who literally fought to keep our navigational routes guarded for those who sailed the Great Lakes. These were truly dedicated, rugged, and solitary men who worked hard to help others.

"Several years later my father was transferred to Raspberry Island, another of the six light stations in the Apostle Island chain. By now I was in high school. I had earned enough money to buy a guitar, and sitting on the end of the Raspberry Island dock, I would sing to the waves that became my audience. I had attempted writing poetry set to music, mostly about the lighthouses and the men who manned these stations. Other times I would watch the campfire glow of my classmates on the mainland three miles away. Foolishly I would call out to them. Days would be filled with swimming and boating—and on one occasion I rowed around the three-quarter-mile-long island.

"On this venture one of the usual sudden storms abruptly caught me close to a rocky and rugged part of the shoreline. The seas swelled and dashed against the huge

(From left) Emma Barningham, Keeper Alva Carpenter, Fran Carpenter, and mother "Marie" on Outer Island about 1935

"This is by East Bay on Outer Island. We took a path through the woods from the lighthouse. We tied our boat here if we were unable to land at the dock during a northwester," Fran explains. Photograph courtesy of Fran Carpenter Platske.

boulders, and the backwash tossed my rowboat about wildly. Guardian angels evidently spirited me away from a watery grave, and later, as I lay exhausted on the pebbled beach after reaching the station, I prayed in thanksgiving.

"Raspberries grew everywhere on this island, and during berry season I picked them by the crate, took them into the village by boat, and sold them for $3.50.

"During the war years, food stamps were issued and patriotism was predominant. Most everyone had a victory garden. Meeting the call to duty, with shovel in hand, I proceeded to dig into the weeds and clay. Several days later a 10 x 10-foot plot was ready for planting. It began blossoming about the time school started, and I rather doubt there was enough harvest for two or three meals. My victory garden undoubtedly finalized its life by succumbing to the clay and weeds.

"It would be too soon now that I would leave the islands behind forever.

"Being an only child, I welcomed the birth of a baby sister this year and the following year, an infant brother. In 1939 the U.S. Lighthouse Service was abolished and ultimately placed under the jurisdiction of the U.S. Coast Guard. Due to failing health,

Father was transferred to a mainland station in Michigan.

"Regretting that the little ones would never know nature as I had, I left my hometown to seek adventure beyond the little village of Bayfield.

"For my twenty-fifth wedding anniversary, my husband planned a surprise trip back to Bayfield and Raspberry Island. I was so overwhelmed with joy, you would think I was going to Europe. When we got there, I soon learned that the caretaker and his wife of Raspberry Island were former friends—I had taken care of their children years before when I first learned to earn money needed for room and board. They offered to take us with them for the day. We rode around the island, stopping at the sandy beach where I had swum years before. Once again I sat on the sun-bleached logs burying my feet in the hot white sand that had been one of the joys of my teen years.

"While I ventured down the beach in search of pretty stones, my husband, Emil, busied himself. When I came back from exploring, he had a surprise awaiting me. There was an old birch tree I had once played under, not too far from the beach. He had carved his and my initials in the tree, which even included an old yellow bit of roping tied about its trunk, obviously left by a previous visitor.

"The years have long gone by, yet the roots of my being are still buried deep among those islands. I knew where every sandbar and boulder lay close beneath the surging waters, where the best wild berries could be found, heard the sound of wailing wind and laughing loons, and saw the soaring eagles high atop the jack pines. Lingering pictures remain there, too, of Great Lakes steamers—their huge stacks leaving written trails of brown smoke across a sinking sun, and Father silhouetted against the horizon as he lowered the American flag on the cliff. Unforgettable will be the scenes of meteors flashing across the great white Milky Way, the exotic dancing of the northern lights, and most of all, falling asleep watching the rays of the lighthouse fingering its beams through a foggy and rainy night and listening to the cry of that lone timber wolf ... and the endless moods of Lake

The tramway at Outer Island Light Station
On Outer Island and other remote light stations where a horse or car was not available, tramways were used to move supplies from the dock up the steep incline to the lighthouse and keepers' dwellings. The Outer Island tramway is still in working condition. Photograph courtesy of Fran Carpenter Platske

Superior, the ways of nature, the clean air, pure water ... the calm and peace.

"To the Apostle Islands, the 'Emerald Crown Jewels' of Lake Superior, for me there will never be a final farewell."

In 1985 Fran again returned to Outer Island, almost fifty years after striking out on her own. Fran wrote in her journal, "Once again I had the opportunity to stand on that platform high atop the proud tower of the Outer Island Lighthouse and gaze across Great Lake Superior. As I stood there, just listening to the peace and quiet, I could once again hear those familiar sounds—sounds of the universe. I imagined I could hear the sound of that laughing loon that Mother and I use to imitate, the squawking of the seagulls, and the cries of the timber wolves filling the night air. I imagined that I could see soaring bald eagles, Canadian sunsets, Great Lakes freighters, heat waves, and summer mirages that would come zooming in as though one could walk around the dwellings at Devil's Island eighteen miles away. And at night, on rare occasions, those awesome, magnificent colorful and resounding northern lights, the aurora borealis. And what lighthouse keeper's child would not recall the rays of the lighthouse beacon forcing their way through the night? Sometimes rain, sometimes fog.

Watercolor of Outer Island Lighthouse painted by Fran Carpenter Platske

When Fran was in the third grade, her father became keeper of the light station on Outer Island, the northeasternmost of the twenty-two Apostle Islands in Lake Superior. Though she was sad at first to say good-bye to her friends in Minnesota, Fran fell in love with Wisconsin's Outer Island and has remained bonded to its beauty and shaped by its spiritual influence. "It is from Outer Island that I have come to firmly believe that there is a compelling bond between the ways of nature and our own human behavior. It's all tied together, and I wouldn't change my life of living on that island, so remote from the mainland, for anything in this whole world."

And yes, the deep-throated boom of a fog signal! Then too, Lake Superior, with its wide spectrum of moods—gentle as a lamb, wild as an angry lion, and sometimes seemingly slumbering beneath a blanket of gray fog; ever so gentle waves, rippling along the shoreline, and again, back to the sound of that laughing loon.

"Sounds of the universe—that abounding network of interwoven restless energy, everywhere and in everything. It is from Outer Island that I have come to firmly believe that there is a compelling bond between the ways of nature and our very own human behavior. I truly believe it is all tied together ... and I wouldn't change my life of living on that island, so remote from the mainland, for anything in this whole world."

In 1993 when Fran and her husband, Emil, again returned to Outer Island, Lake Superior was up to her old tricks. The day began with blue skies and brilliant sun. About 15 miles out, fog silently crept in and enshrouded the lake. Next fresh winds challenged their boat's headway and finally gave birth to 5-foot waves. The lake became a bucking bronco. By the time the boat reached Outer Island, landing was tentative. The National Park Service staff member made a brilliant docking. Fran and Emil gratefully debarked and climbed the working tramway to the lighthouse.

Fran has captured the essence of the nature that surrounded her as an island light-house child in her watercolor paintings and poems, including the one below.

Farewell to Outer Island
From We, the Keepers' Kids and the Old Lighthouse Service
by Fran Carpenter Platske

The Apostle Islands are in mid Lake Superior,
There are twenty-two of them as I recall ...
There are six lighthouses among these beautiful isles,
Outer Island most remote of them all.

Now the towering lighthouse on Outer Island,
Was our home for five years and then,
We were transferred to the lighthouse on Raspberry Island,
Never to see this lighthouse again.

So the last night on Outer I stood on that high cliff,
Where the tramway steps down to the shore,
And the sounds of the universe communed with my soul,
Like they never had done before!

It wasn't a sudden awakening,
It was more like a melodious, unwritten tune ...
'Twas in the cries of the timber wolves that filled the night air,
And in the distance, the song of a loon!

It was in the wind that swept cross that Great Lake Superior,
The waters responded with their song,
As they lapped the white sand beach, splashed on the rocks,
Then forever, both would move on.

The music played on in the millions of stars
Where profound silence ruled all on high,
Then as though a great maestro had lifted his hand,
A meteor blazed 'cross the night sky!

But I too would remember when the wind would rage
And the waters leap to the dark clouds above,
Forgetting they had once gently mingled together,
Not remembering their own song of love.

The thunder would boom—there would be torrents of rain,
Tongues of lightning lashed out into space,
Like the clash of giant cymbals and the roll of great drums,
Awesome power met—face to face!

Oh—but the storm would subside as though weary of war,
Silence would then take command,
A velvety fog parted the sea and the sky
Until sunshine warmed all the land.

Dewdrops would sparkle on a spider's fine web,
A fly dried off one fragile wing,
Buttercups and daisies reached for the sun,
And all around, Mother Nature would sing!

I'd also remember those magnificent sights,
Rarely seen on warm summer nights,
When spasms of colors that leaped to the heavenly gates,
Revealing the great northern lights–the aurora borealis!

Then all of a sudden, bank swallows twittered by,
Once again I heard the timber wolves' cries,
The squawk of a seagull–the song of that loon,
My soul knew ... we were all saying good-bye.

I realize now how much I had learned from the
Sights and the sounds that were there,
There is a network of power, restless energy that is endless
And abounds in everything ... everywhere!

It is in the wind, the sea, the call of the wild,
You and me to the warm sun above,
But the greatest power that nurtures it all,
Is the unseen power ... of love!

Yes, this had been my playground, this had been my stage,
Free, where earth put on her greatest shows,
I saw and heard the universe sing,
I had a seat in the very front row!

In prayer I go back to that high cliff on Outer
And walk where my footsteps once trod ...
My soul joins the wind and is refreshed by the sea,
Then returns through the Spirit of God.

I pray too, Dear Lord, when my soul soars to heaven,
May I have a seat in the very front row?
I'd like to be with the angels and sing in their choir,
To the souls on earth below.

(Standing) Keeper Alva G. Carpenter and his wife, Marie; (kneeling) Assistant Keeper Vern Barningham, Fran Carpenter, and Emma Barningham on Outer Island about 1936

Photograph courtesy of Fran Carpenter Platske

May I be in the wind and the sounds of the sea,
And in the sun that warms from above,
Giving strength to souls as was given to me,
Through your ... Supreme Power of Love!

Oh yes, it is ... all tied together!

Fran Carpenter Platske had come home to Outer Island as an older child, grateful for the gifts she had been given—and determined to share them with others. Fran was one of the original founders of the Great Lakes Lighthouse Keepers Association and the Lake Superior Lighthouse Keeper Family Organization. She continues to take an active role in lighthouse preservation.

FAMILY RECIPES

Fran says, "One summer when I was eleven or twelve years old, I decided to bake my mother's Lazy Daisy cake while my mother and father went ashore to get the mail and supplies. When I mixed the powdered sugar with water to make the frosting, I didn't realize that I needed only a small amount of water—I used two and a half boxes of powdered sugar (all my mother had on hand) and still had a watery mixture. I placed a generous handful of fresh-picked wild strawberries atop the "frosted" cake. I was certain it would please my mother when they returned from the mainland—but it didn't!"

Marie Carpenter's Lazy Daisy Cake

1/3 cup milk
1 tablespoon butter
12/3 cup flour
1/2 teaspoon salt

13/4 teaspoons baking powder
1 egg
1 cup sugar
1 teaspoon vanilla

Scald milk and add butter; let cool to lukewarm. Combine flour, salt, and baking powder.

Beat egg slightly, and gradually add sugar, beating constantly until thick and lemon colored; add vanilla. Alternately add small amounts of milk mixture and dry ingredients mixture, mixing lightly but thoroughly.

Pour batter into greased pan, and bake at 350° for 30 to 40 minutes. Let cake cool, and frost with powdered sugar frosting.

Fran has passed on her mother's Skillet Spaghetti recipe to her grown children, and her husband, Emil, often makes it for his hunting companions during deer season.

MARIE CARPENTER'S SKILLET SPAGHETTI

1 pound hamburger
1 onion, chopped
1 green pepper, chopped fine
1 can tomatoes
2 cups water

1 cup uncooked spaghetti
1 teaspoon salt
1 teaspoon paprika
1/2 teaspoon pepper

Brown hamburger in a large skillet. Add onion and green pepper; add remaining ingredients. Bake at 350° for about 1 hour.

OUTER ISLAND LIGHT STATION is part of the Apostle Islands National Lakeshore. The national lakeshore headquarters is in the old county courthouse in Bayfield, Wisconsin. The museum and bookstore staffs at the headquarters can provide visitor information. The Apostle Island Cruise Service, a private contractor, offers daily cruises to the Apostle Islands lighthouse stations, including Raspberry Island, which has been restored and is manned by docents in period dress. Call 715/779-3398 before visiting to confirm that the site is accessible.

AFTERWORD

These lighthouse "children" have graciously shared their memories, giving all of us—as well as future generations—rare glimpses of a gone-forever way of life. Each of these children shows individual strength and character, yet they share some common characteristics. For instance, all of them helped with the daily chores of tending a light station, including doing some hard physical labor, and the more responsibilities they were given, the more they felt like assistant keepers. Like their parents, many of these lighthouse children sported rough hands and "weeping" knees from the endless scrubbing, polishing, sweeping, chopping wood, washing clothes, and myriad other everyday chores done to keep the light stations in white-glove condition. And today many of these children keep their homes in the same pristine condition—just in case the lighthouse inspector drops by unexpectedly.

Even though these children grew up at remote, isolated light stations, they were expected to keep up with their school lessons. Some of them were tutored by their parents and others by government-provided teachers or correspondence courses. Some lived close enough—that is, within an hour or two's commute by boat, horse, or car—to attend a public school. Others lived with relatives and friends on the mainland during the school year, which sometimes meant working to earn room and board and always meant weeks—or months—of separation from their keeper fathers.

Despite periods of separation, family ties usually remained strong. Lighthouse daughters seemed to form especially strong bonds with their fathers. The girls revered their fathers, enjoyed working alongside them, and unquestioningly obeyed them. June Dudley Watts recalled that when she was growing up the rule was "What Dad says is what goes."

Another common experience for these lighthouse children was seeing nature's fury firsthand. Some of them watched helplessly as floodwaters swept away family belongings—including animals. Many of them say that the stormier the weather, the safer everyone felt in being together as a family. "I don't remember a storm when we felt threatened," Anna Bowen Hoge states matter of factly. "When there was a bad Lake Superior storm brewing, Dad secured everything and Mom and us kids made taffy. We just pulled and pulled that taffy until all settled down." "I love a good nor'easter," John Gaskill says emphatically. "It reminds me of being at the lighthouse." And to this day, Diana Owens Brown heads to the beach whenever the weather turns stormy.

These children grew up knowing that survival depended upon the family working together. They learned not to expect anything unless it was earned. They knew how to make do with what they had and to depend on their own wits. They learned to appreciate nature and the beauty of the earth–and they learned to respect the danger of cliffs and the power of water. They lost family members and pets to natural disasters, and they learned to treasure life. They shared their fathers' deep sense of responsibility in keeping the lighthouse lamp burning properly to provide both guidance and comfort to all mariners passing their way.

Their stories record firsthand vignettes of American history from the advent of the use of Fresnel lenses in lighthouses and the proportional growth of our nation's shipping, to the coming of paved highways and the subsequent decline in the use of waterways, to the invention of solar-powered lights and radar navigation and the extinction of flame and keeper. They saw the stately dark blue of the U.S. Lighthouse Service uniforms replaced by the U.S. Coast Guard's sterile military white. They saw meticulously kept logbooks tossed into boxes, carefully polished lenses dismantled, and their beloved childhood homes stripped of U.S. Lighthouse Service-issued items that were labeled "surplus."

But none of these life-changing events diminished their love of lighthouses. Like other lighthouse children, many of these "children" still live within the range of the light of one of the stations their parents served. And like many other keepers' children, they actively support preservation and restoration efforts and serve as interpreters, telling visitors what they experienced when their family made a light station their home.

I cannot thank each of these "children" enough for sharing their stories so openly with me so I could share them with others. Their memories are now our memories.

–Cheryl Shelton-Roberts

BIBLIOGRAPHY

Bureau of Lighthouses. *U.S. Lighthouse Service Bulletins.* Washington, D.C.: Government Printing Office, 1912-39.

Clifford, Candace. *Inventory of Historic Light Stations.* Washington, D.C.: National Park Service, Division of History, 1994.

Gibbs, Jim A. *Lighthouses of the Pacific.* West Chester, Penn.: Schiffer Publishing Ltd., 1986.

Hickam, Homer. *Torpedo Junction.* Baltimore: Navy Institute Press, 1989.

Holland, F. Ross Jr. *Great American Lighthouses.* Washington, D.C.: The Preservation Press, 1994.

——. *A History of Cape Hatteras Light Station.* Washington, D.C.: National Park Service, Division of History, 1968.

Hyde, Charles K. *The Northern Lights: Lighthouses of the Upper Great Lakes.* Lansing, Mich.: Two Peninsula Press, 1990.

Jones, Dorothy Holder, and Ruth Sexton Sargent. *The Original Biography of Abbie Burgess Lighthouse Heroine.* Self-published, 1992.

Kochel, Kenneth G. *America's Atlantic Coast Lighthouses: A Traveler's Guide.* Florida: Betken Publications, 1996.

Livingston, Dewey, and Dave Snow. *The History and Architecture of the Point Reyes Light Station.* Washington, D.C.: National Park Service, 1990.

Platske, Fran Carpenter. *We, the Keepers' Kids and the Old Lighthouse Service.* Kalamazoo, Mich.: Self-published, 1995.

Putnam, George R. "Beacons of the Sea; Lighting the Coast of the United States," *National Geographic Magazine,* January 1936.

Roberts, Bruce, and Ray Jones. *Eastern Great Lakes Lighthouses.* Old Saybrook, Conn.: Globe Pequot Press, 1996.

——. *Mid-Atlantic Lighthouses.* Old Saybrook, Conn.: Globe Pequot Press, 1996.

——. *New England Lighthouses.* Old Saybrook, Conn.: Globe Pequot Press, 1996.

——. *Southern Lighthouses.* Old Saybrook, Conn.: Globe Pequot Press, 1994.

——. *Western Great Lakes Lighthouses.* Old Saybrook, Conn.: Globe Pequot Press, 1996.

——. *Western Lighthouses.* Old Saybrook, Conn.: Globe Pequot Press, 1993.

Shanks, Ralph, and Lisa Woo Shanks, ed. *Guardians of the Golden Gate.* Petaluma, Calif.: Costaño Books, 1990.

Shelton-Roberts, Cheryl. "Cape Hatteras: Last Family Member Leaves the Lighthouse." *Lighthouse News,* Vol. 1, No. 2, 1995.

——. "Light Years Away." Lighthouse News, Vol. 2., No. 1, 1996.

Snow, Edward Rowe. *Famous Lighthouses of New England.* Boston: The Yankee Publishing Company, 1945.

Stick, David. *Graveyard of the Atlantic: Shipwrecks of the North Carolina Coast.* Chapel Hill, N.C.: The University of North Carolina Press, 1952.

——. *North Carolina Lighthouses.* Raleigh, N.C.: Division of Archives and History, North

Carolina Department of Cultural Resources, 1992.

United States Department of the Interior. *1994 Inventory of Historic Light Stations.* Washington, D.C.: Cultural Resources History Division, 1994.

United States Light-House Board. *Annual Reports of U.S. Light-House Board.* Government Printing Office, Washington, D.C.: U.S. Light-House Board, 1872, 1890, 1903, 1914.

United States Lighthouse Service. *List of Beacons, Buoys and Day-Marks in the Fifth Light-House District.* Washington, D.C.: Government Printing Office, 1897.

United States Lighthouse Service. *U.S. Lighthouse Service Bulletins.* Washington, D.C.: Government Printing Office, 1912-1939.

Wallace, David H. *Principal Keeper's Quarters Cape Hatteras Light Station.* Harpers Ferry Center, W.Va.: National Park Service, 1991.

Weiss, George. *The Lighthouse Service: Its History, Activities and Organization.* Baltimore: The Johns Hopkins Press, 1926.

Wheeler, Wayne C., ed. "Letters to the Keep'." *The Keeper's Log,* Vol 9, No. 3, Spring 1993.

Witney, Dudley. *The Lighthouse.* Canada: New York Graphic Society, Little, Brown and Company, 1975.

INDEX

Here are some other books from Pineapple Press on related topics. For a complete catalog, write to Pineapple Press, P.O. Box 3889, Sarasota, Florida 34230-3889, or call (800) 746-3275. Or visit our website at www.pineapplepress.com.

Guardians of the Lights, Revised Edition, by Elinor De Wire. Stories of the heroism and fortitude of the men and women of the U.S. Lighthouse Service, who kept vital shipping lanes safe from 1716 until early in the 20th century.

The Lightkeepers' Menagerie by Elinor De Wire. The author has been writing about lighthouses since 1972. During that time she found that hundreds of lighthouse animals wandered into her research notes and photo collection. This book is the story of all these cold-nosed, whiskered, woolly, hoofed, horned, feathered, and finned keepers of the lights.

Guide to Florida Lighthouses by Elinor De Wire. The updated edition of this book traces the history of each of Florida's lighthouses. It is also a guidebook for those who wish to visit these beacons, complete with maps, visiting hours, and addresses for additional information.

Florida Lighthouses for Kids by Elinor De Wire. Learn about the people who designed and built Florida's lighthouses, meet some of the keepers, see how lighthouses operate, find out about their new roles as museums, and more. Ages 9 and up.

Lighthouses of Greece by Elinor De Wire and Dolores Reyes-Pergioudakis. This lavishly illustrated and carefully researched book covers more than 100 lighthouses, most still guiding ships around the Greek Islands.

Lighthouse Ghosts, Second Edition, by Norma Elizabeth and Bruce Roberts. Here are 13 tales of specters that haunt lighthouses from California to Massachusetts, Michigan to Florida. Meet the lighthouse keepers who took their obligation so seriously that they continue to make their rounds and keep the lights burning long after they're gone.

Lighthouse Ghosts and Carolina Coastal Legends, Second Edition, by Norma Elizabeth and Bruce Roberts. From the Graveyard of the Atlantic to beautiful Hilton Head Island, lighthouse legends abound. A black pelican, a "gray" man, and a young girl with misty-blue eyes have been warning locals of hurricanes for centuries. Includes complete visiting information with phone numbers, addresses, and websites.

CPSIA information can be obtained
at www.ICGtesting.com
Printed in the USA
BVOW06s1914160317
478380BV00005B/3/P